Original French edition:
"Les 5 blessures qui empêchent d'être soi-même"
First printing: 2000.
CAN ISBN 2-920932-18-7

Copyright © 2001 by Lise Bourbeau
First edition
National library of Canada
National library of Quebec
ISBN 2-920932-21-7

Distributor
Lotus Brands Inc.
P.O. Box 325
Twin Lakes, WI
53181 USA
Tel: 262-889-8501 or 1-800-824-6396
Fax: 262-889-2461
email: lotuspress@lotuspress.com
www.lotuspress.com

Publisher
Les Editions E.T.C. Inc.
1102 Boul. La Salette
Bellefeuille (Quebec)
J0R 1A0   Canada
Tel: 450-431-5336; Fax: 450-431-0991
Email: info@leseditionsetc.com
www.leseditionsetc.com

LISE BOURBEAU

BEST-SELLING AUTHOR

"LISTEN TO YOUR BODY, your best friend on Earth"

rejection

abandonment

injustice

Heal your wounds & find your true

humiliation

betrayal

Finally, a book that explains why it's so hard being yourself!

ÉDITIONS E.T.C. INC

Acknowledgments

From the bottom of my heart, I would like to thank the thousands of people I've worked with over the years, without whom my research on the wounds and masks would have been impossible

I particularly want to thank all those who have done the course on "Efficient Techniques for Counseling." Thanks to their ability to reveal themselves completely, the subject matter used in this book was greatly enriched. Very special thanks to the members of the "Listen to Your Body" team who took part in my research and who supplied me with several elements in this book. Thanks to all of you, my passion for research and for elaborating new synthesis is still very much alive.

Furthermore, a big thank you to those who directly contributed to the writing of this book, starting with my husband Jacques, who made the hours spent writing this book easier simply by being there, then Monica Bourbeau Shields, Odette Pelletier, Micheline St-Jacques, Nathalie Raymond and Michèle Derrudder who all did a great job correcting the manuscript and finally Claudie Ogier and Elisa Palazzo, illustrators.

Contents

Preface

Writing this book would never have been possible without the perseverance of several researchers who, like me, didn't hesitate to make the fruit of their research and syntheses public, in spite of the controversy and the scepticism that their work provoked. Moreover, researchers know that in general, they'll be criticized, as will their publications, and they prepare themselves to confront this. They are motivated by those who accept their discoveries and by the idea of helping human beings evolve. The first of the researchers I would like to thank is the Austrian psychiatrist Sigmund Freud for his monumental discovery of the subconscious and for having dared to state that there could be a link between the physique and the emotional and mental dimensions of a human being.

I would then like to thank one of his students, Wilhelm Reich, who in my opinion was the great forerunner of metaphysics. He was the first man to really establish a link between psychology and physiology by proving that neurosis affected both the mental state and the physical body.

After that, John C. Pierrakos[1] and Alexander Lowen, both psychiatrists and students of Wilhelm Reich, who

---

1   Author and founder of CORE ENERGETICS, Life Rhythm Publication.

created bio-energy, which established that the will to be cured implicated the physical body of patients as much as their emotions and thoughts.

It is, above all, thanks to the work of John Pierrakos and his companion Eva Brooks that I was able to elaborate the synthesis that you will discover in this book. In 1992, I went to a very interesting course given by Barry Walker, a student of John Pierrakos, and since then I have observed and researched extensively to complete my synthesis of the five wounds and the masks that accompany them. Moreover, because of the thousands of people who have attended my workshops and my own personal experiences, everything that is described in this book has been the object of countless verifications since that date.

There is no scientific proof for what I advance in this book but, before rejecting it, I invite you to check out this synthesis yourself, especially as you may find it will help you to improve your quality of life.

If you are reading one of my books for the first time and you aren't familiar with the teachings of LISTEN TO YOUR BODY, some of the expressions I use may leave you feeling perplexed. For example, I make a clear distinction between sentiment and emotion, intellect and intelligence, mastering and controlling. The sense that I give to these words is explained in detail in my other books and in my workshops.

Everything that is written is directed as much at men as at women. When it's not the case, it's specified. I also continue to use the word GOD. I remind you that when I speak of GOD, I'm referring to your SUPERIOR SELF, your real self, the SELF who knows what it really needs to live in love, happiness, harmony, peace, health, abundance and joy. I hope you have as much pleasure discovering yourself in the following chapters as I have sharing my discoveries.

With love,

Lise Bourbeau

Chapter 1

The creation of wounds and masks

Before we are born, our inner GOD attracts our soul to the environment and to the family we will need during this lifetime. This magnetic attraction and its objectives are determined, on the one hand, by what we haven't yet managed to experience with love and acceptance in our previous lives and, on the other hand, by what our future parents have to solve through us. Our souls choose our parents and the circumstances of our birth for very precise reasons. What's more, we know when we come into this life that we have certain experiences to live out, certain wounds to heal, and have chosen the parents and environments to help us. This is why children and parents often have the same wounds to heal. We also know we must stay in touch with our true selves while living and transforming our life experiences. We all have the same mission: *to live our life experiences until we manage to accept them and discover and love ourselves through them.*

We can always count on our inner GOD to help us. HE is omniscient (knows everything), omnipresent (is everywhere) and omnipotent (all-powerful). This power is always present and at work within us, guiding us to the people and situations we need to grow and evolve according to the life path that was chosen before birth. When we are born, we are no longer conscious of our past, because we concentrate above all on the needs of our soul in this lifetime. The soul wants us to accept ourselves with what we have acquired, with our failings, strengths, weaknesses, desires, and our personality.

When we do not accept ourselves or our experiences, if in other words we continue to feel guilty, ashamed, afraid, judge ourselves in any way, or exhibit any other form of non-acceptance, we will continually attract other circumstances and people to make us relive the same experience. Some of us will not only live the same experience several times throughout our lives, we may also have to be reincarnated several times before we reach complete acceptance.

Accepting an experience doesn't mean it is our preference or that we agree with it. It rather means allowing ourselves to experiment and learn through experience. We must especially learn to recognize what is beneficial for us and what isn't. The only way to do that is to become conscious of the consequences of each experience. There are consequences to everything we decide or don't decide, everything we do or don't do, everything we say or don't say, and even to what we think and feel.

As human beings, we want to learn and grow intelligently through life, so when we realize that an experience can have harmful consequences, rather than blaming ourselves or others, we must simply accept that we chose it (perhaps unconsciously) so we could learn that it wasn't a 'smart' or beneficial experience, and not one to be repeated. We'll then remember that experience, and benefit from it another time. That's what we call accepting the experiences we live through. You may have to allow yourself to repeat the same mistake or live through the same unpleasant experience several times. I would like to remind you that even if you say: *"I never want to go through that again,"* it will be likely to come back until you have gained the necessary experience and willpower to transform it. Why don't we understand the first time around? Because our egos, supported by our beliefs, get in the way.

We all have beliefs that prevent us from being what we want to be. The more these attitudes or beliefs hurt us, the more we try to shut them out. We even manage to believe that they no longer belong to us. We therefore have to be incarnated several times before we manage to accept them. Only when our mental, emotional and physical bodies listen to our inner GOD will our soul be completely happy.

Everything we experience without acceptance accumulates in the soul. As the soul is immortal, it continually comes back in different human forms, bringing along its accumulated soul memory. Before we are born, we decide why we want to come back, and what we want to solve in our next incarnation. This decision, and all that we have accumulated in the past, is not recorded in our conscious memory (the memory based on intellect). It is only as time goes by that we gradually become conscious of our life path and of what we have to solve.

Whenever I speak of something "unsolved" I'm referring to an experience lived through without acceptance of the self. There is a big difference between accepting an experience and accepting the self. Let's take the example of a little girl who was rejected by her father because he wanted a boy. In such a case, accepting the experience consists in giving the father the right to have wanted a boy and reject his daughter. To accept *herself,* this little girl must give herself the right to resent her father and forgive herself for having resented him. She must carry no judgement towards her father or towards herself; only compassion and understanding for the suffering of both of them.

She will know that this experience is completely solved when she in turn will reject someone without accusing herself; she will have only compassion and understanding for her actions.

Don't let your ego fool you. It often does everything possible to try to make you believe you have worked through a situation. There are often moments when we say to ourselves: *"Yes, I understand why the other person acts like that"* so that we don't have to look at and forgive ourselves. Our ego always tries to find a way to put aside unpleasant situations. Sometimes we accept a situation or a person without having forgiven ourselves or without even having allowed ourselves to blame that other person. That's called *"simply accepting the experience."* I repeat: it's important to see the difference between accepting an experience and accepting *ourselves.* It's difficult to reach this acceptance because our ego doesn't want to admit that the only reason we go through difficult experiences is to make us aware that we do the same thing to others.

16

Have you ever realized that when you accuse someone of something, that person often accuses you of the
same thing?

It's so important to learn to know and accept ourselves as much as possible; that's how we will reduce the
number of experiences that cause us to suffer. It's up to us
to decide to become the master of our lives rather than letting our ego control us. It requires a lot of courage to face
all this, because old wounds will inevitably be re-opened,
causing suffering - especially if they are wounds we've
had for several lives. The more we suffer in a given situation or with a given person, the more deep-rooted the
problem.

We all need to accept ourselves just as we are, with
all our failings and strengths. Shortly after our birth, however, we realize that when we are being ourselves, we often unsettle the adults in our world and those who are
close to us. We therefore assume that being natural is not
good, not right. This discovery is painful, and children often express this pain through fits of anger. These outbursts
have become so frequent that we now believe that they're
normal. We call them 'childhood crises' or 'teenage crises.' These fits of anger have perhaps become normal for
humans, but they are certainly not natural. Children who
act naturally, who are balanced and who have the right to
be themselves don't have "fits" like these. Unfortunately,
there are very few 'natural' children. I have observed that
most children go through the four following stages:

After having experienced the joy of being themselves, which is the first stage in their existence, they ex-

perience the pain of not being allowed to be themselves - the second stage. This is followed by a period of rage and rebellion - the third stage. Then, to reduce the pain, children create a new personality to become what others want them to be - the fourth stage. Some people remain in the third stage all their lives; they are always reacting, angry, or in trouble.

During the third and fourth stages, we create several masks (new personalities) that we use to protect us from the suffering endured during the second stage. There are five such masks and they correspond to the five great fundamental wounds inflicted on humans. The observations I've made over several years have enabled me to realize that all human suffering can be condensed into five wounds. Here they are in chronological order; that is to say, in the order they appear in life.

REJECTION

ABANDONMENT

HUMILIATION

BETRAYAL

INJUSTICE

Each time we suffer or cause suffering because of these wounds, our whole being feels betrayed. We are not being faithful to our inner GOD, to the needs of our being; because we let our ego, with its beliefs and fears, control our life. We create masks to *hide*, from ourselves or from others, what we haven't yet wanted to solve.

What are these masks? Here they are, accompanied by the wounds they're trying to hide.

WOUND	MASK
Rejection	Withdrawal
Abandonment	Dependence
Humiliation	Masochism (emotional/mental)
Betrayal	Control
Injustice	Rigidity

The strength of the mask depends on the depth of the wound. A mask represents a person with a specific character type, because numerous beliefs, influencing the attitude and the behavior of the person, are developed for each mask. The deeper the wound, the more we will suffer and the more we will wear our mask.

We only wear a mask when we want to protect ourselves. For example, those who feel that an event was unjust, or who judge themselves as being unjust, or who fear others will judge them as being unjust, will wear the mask of *rigidity*; that is to say, they will adopt the behavior of a rigid person.

Here is an image that will better illustrate the way a wound and its corresponding mask are linked. The inner wound can be compared to a physical wound that you have had on your hand for a long time. You have always ignored this wound and have never tended to it. In fact, you preferred to wrap a bandage around it so that you wouldn't see it. That bandage is equivalent to a mask. You thought that you could pretend you weren't hurt. Do you really think that's the solution? Of course not. We all know that, but the ego doesn't. That's one way it fools us.

Now let's imagine that even though your hand is bandaged, every time someone touches it, it really hurts. Someone, out of love, takes your hand - but you react by shouting: *"Ouch! You're hurting me!"* You can imagine how surprised that person will be. Did they really want to hurt you? No, because if your hand hurts when someone touches it, it's only because you have not tended to your wound. The other person is not responsible for your suffering.

It's the same for all wounds: We so often feel rejected, abandoned, betrayed, humiliated or unjustly treated. In fact, we feel hurt because our ego likes to make us believe that someone else is to blame, so we look for a culprit. Sometimes we decide that we're that culprit, but that's no truer than blaming someone else. You know there are no guilty people; there are only people who suffer. I know now that the more we accuse (ourselves or others), the more the same experience repeats itself. Accusations are only good for making humans unhappy whereas, when we start looking with compassion at the part of the human that is suffering, events, situations and people begin to transform themselves.

The masks we create to protect ourselves are visible in our morphology, in our physical appearance. People often ask me if it's possible to detect wounds in young children. Personally, I enjoy observing my seven grandsons who, at the time of writing these lines, are between seven months and nine years old. I can already see wounds beginning to show in the physical appearance of most of them. Wounds that can be easily seen at that age indicate wounds that are deep-set. On the other hand, I have observed that the adult bodies of two of my three children show different wounds than those I saw when they were children and teenagers.

The body is so intelligent that it always finds a way to let us know what we have to solve. In fact, our inner GOD uses our body to communicate with us.

In the following chapters, you will discover how to recognize your masks and those of others. In the last chapter I speak of what we need to do to heal wounds that have, up to now, been neglected and consequently what we need to do to stop suffering. The masks that hide these wounds will then naturally be transformed.

Moreover, it is important not to take literally the words used to express the wounds or the masks. Someone can be rejected and suffer from *injustice*; someone else can be betrayed and feel rejected; another person can be abandoned and suffer from *humiliation*, etc.

All this will be clearer for you once you have read the description of each wound and the accompanying characteristics.

The five types described in this book may seem similar to those described in other character studies. Each study is different and this one wasn't made with the intention of doing away with or of replacing those that were done in the past. One of these studies, carried out by the psychologist Gérard Heymans nearly a hundred years ago, is still popular today. In his study, there are eight character types: the passionate, the angry, the nervous, the sentimental, the fiery, the phlegmatic, the apathetic and the amorphous type. When he uses the word passionate to describe a certain type of person, that doesn't mean that the other types can't experience passion in their lives. Each word used to describe the character types is in fact used to describe the dominant character of a person. I therefore repeat that you mustn't take the literal sense of the words.

It's possible that, when reading the description of each wound, together with the behavior and the attitude of the corresponding masks, you will recognize yourself in each one of them. I really must stress the importance of observing the physical body because this is what faithfully reflects what is happening inside of us - it's much harder to recognize ourselves on the emotional and mental planes. Remember that our ego doesn't want us to discover all our beliefs because it survives with our feeding it with our beliefs. I won't explain further the ego in this book because I speak about it in detail in my books *Listen to Your Body, Your Best Friend on Earth* and *Listen to Your Body, Part 2.*

You may well react and even resist when you read that people suffering from a certain wound are reacting to a certain parent. I did research with thousands of people before coming to that conclusion. I'll say what I say in each of my workshops: it's the parent we liked best when we were teenagers with whom we have the most to solve. It's absolutely normal to find it difficult to accept that we hold a grudge against the parent we love most. The first reaction to this is generally denial, followed by anger after which we are ready to face reality - the start of the healing process.

You may find the description of the behavior and the attitudes that are linked to the different wounds negative. When you recognize one of your wounds, you may there-fore find yourself reacting to the description of the mask you created to avoid suffering. This resistance is normal and human. Give yourself time. Remember, when your mask is in control, you are not yourself, and the same goes for everyone around you. Don't you find it reassuring to know that when someone else's behavior bothers you or upsets you, it's a sign that they have put on their masks to avoid suffering? If you keep that in mind, you will be more tolerant and it'll be easier for you to love them. Let's take the example of a teenager who acts tough. If you know that he acts like that to hide his vulnerability and fear, you can have a different relationship with him be-cause you'll know that he is neither tough nor dangerous. You'll keep calm and will even be able to see his qualities rather than be afraid and see only his failings.

I find it encouraging knowing that even if the wounds we were born with are regularly activated by our reaction to the people and circumstances that surround us, the masks that we created to protect ourselves are not permanent. If you put into practice the healing methods suggested in the last chapter, you will see your masks gradually become smaller and, consequently, your attitude change. Your body may also change. It could, however, be several years before results are visible in the physical body because the body changes more slowly due to the tangible matter it's made of.

Our subtle bodies (emotional and mental) take less time to change once a decision has really been made out of love. For example, it's very easy to wish for (emotional) and to imagine (mental) yourself visiting another country. The decision to go on that trip can be made in a few minutes. It will, however, take much longer to plan and organize everything, to save enough money, to finalize the arrangements in the physical world.

One good way to check your physical transformation is to have your photo taken each year. Have close-ups made of all the parts of your body so that you can see the details easily. It's true that some people change more rapidly than others. What is important is to continue to work on your inner transformation because that's what will make you a happier person in life.

While reading the next five chapters, I suggest you write down everything that seems to correspond to you and then re-read the chapter or chapters that best describe your attitude and above all, your physical appearance.

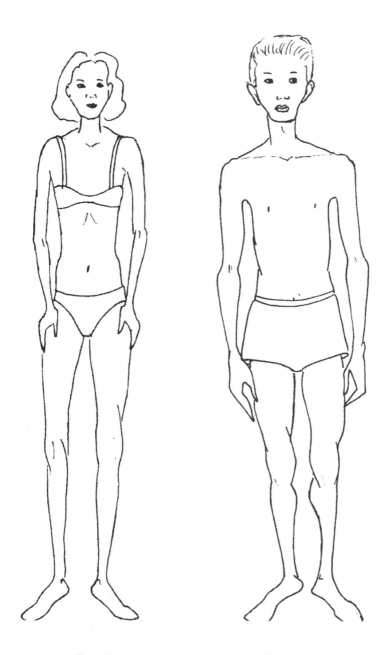

**Body of a person suffering
from the wound of REJECTION
(Mask of Withdrawal)**

Chapter 2

Rejection

Let's have a look at the words "rejection" or "to reject." The dictionary gives us several definitions:

> ***To throw out***
> ***To rebuff***
> ***To repel***
> ***Intolerance***
> ***To deny***
> ***To evacuate***

Many people find it difficult to see the difference between "to reject" and "to abandon." To abandon someone is to move away from that person for something or someone else, whereas to reject someone is to push *him or her* away, not wanting that person at our side or in our life. When we reject we use the expression *"I don't want to"* while the person who abandons says, *"I can't."*

Rejection is a very deep wound because those who suffer from it feel that not only their whole being, but also their right to exist is being rejected. It is the first of the five wounds to emerge, which means that it is present very early in life. The soul that comes back to earth to heal this wound will experience *rejection* from birth, and in several cases, even before.

Let's take the example of unwanted babies, babies that arrive "by accident," as the saying goes. If these babies' souls haven't already dealt with *rejection* - if in other words, they haven't managed to be happy and to be themselves in spite of it, they will inevitably experience *rejection* in this lifetime. An obvious example is that of a baby who is not of the desired sex. There are of course other reasons for which parents reject their children but what is important to realize is that only souls that need to live through this experience will be attracted to one or even two parents who will reject their child.

Often parents have no intention of rejecting their children, but that doesn't stop the children from feeling rejected anyway at the slightest incident, whether that be an unpleasant comment or a parent's impatience or anger. As long as the wound isn't healed, it will very easily be re-activated. People who feel rejected aren't objective. They interpret incidents through the filters of their wound and so feel rejected even when they aren't.

As soon as babies start to feel rejected, they begin to create the mask of WITHDRAWAL. I have attended many regressions where people went back to their fetal stage, and I was able to observe that those who are affected by the wound of *rejection* see themselves as very small in their mother's womb, as taking up very little room, and often as being in the dark. That for me was confirmation that the *withdrawer* mask could be created even before birth.

From now until the end of the book I will use the expression *withdrawers* to refer to people suffering from *rejection*. The *withdrawer* mask is the new personality, the character developed to avoid suffering from *rejection*.

Those with this mask are easily recognizable because of their *withdrawn* physical bodies. It seems that their bodies, or parts of their bodies, want to disappear. The bodies are usually thin and contracted, which makes it easier to disappear or at least to be less present or visible in a group. They are bodies that don't want to take up too much space, just like *withdrawers,* who will spend their lives trying not to take up too much space. When we have the impression that there is almost no flesh on the bones, we can deduce that the wound is even greater.

Withdrawers are people who question their right to exist and who don't seem to be completely incarnated. This explains why their bodies are often fragmented, incomplete. It's as if a piece were missing or as if parts of the body didn't go together. The right side of the body or of the face can, for example, be very different from the left. All this is easily visible. You don't have to measure to know if the two sides are alike. (Remember that it's very rare for the two sides of any body to be identical.)

When I speak of fragmented, incomplete bodies, I'm referring to bodies that give the impression of something missing, such as the buttocks, the breasts, or the chin; or where the ankles are very small. Bodies that have a hollow in the area of the back, the chest, the stomach, etc. also fit into this category.

We can say that a body is *contracted* when it gives the impression that it is turned in towards itself. The shoulders are turned forward and the arms are often close to the body. We also have the impression that the growth of the body or a part of it was stunted. One part of the body might look younger than the rest of it or, when the whole body is contracted, we might think that we're looking at an adult in a child's body.

When you see someone with a deformed body that inspires pity, you can also deduce that person suffers from *rejection*. Moreover, the soul has chosen this type of body before birth to put itself in a propitious situation to overcome this wound.

The face and eyes of *withdrawers* are small. The eyes seem vacant or empty because people suffering from this wound tend to withdraw easily into their own world or to have their heads in the clouds (or experience out - body experiences). The eyes are often full of fear. When looking at *withdrawers'* faces, we may get the impression that we are looking at a mask, especially if there are dark circles around the eyes. They themselves can also have the feeling that they're looking through a mask. Some *withdrawers* have told me that this feeling could last a whole day, whereas for others it lasted only a few minutes. However long it lasts, it's a way for them to avoid suffering by being "absent" when something happens.

Those who have all of the above characteristics have a much deeper wound than those who have only *withdrawer* eyes or *withdrawer* legs, for example. When someone's body shows about 50% of the physical characteristics that distinguish *withdrawers*, we can conclude that this person wears the *withdrawer* mask about 50% of the time. For instance, someone with a fairly large body whose face and eyes are small like those of *withdrawers*, or someone with a fairly large body whose ankles are small. Having just one part of the body that corresponds to the characteristics of a *withdrawer* shows that the wound of rejection is not so deep.

Wearing a mask means we are no longer ourselves. We take on a different attitude, adopted when young, because we believe that this attitude will protect us. The instinctive reaction of someone who feels rejected is to withdraw. Children who create a *withdrawer* mask when feeling rejected are children who very often live in an imaginary world. That's why they are generally good, calm children who don't cause problems and who don't make noise.

Withdrawer children play alone in their imaginary world and build castles in the air. They are even able to believe that their parents were given the wrong baby in the hospital, that they are not their real parents. These children invent different means to escape from home, one of them being their strong desire to go to school. Once at school, however, they will have their heads in the clouds and will withdraw into their own world, especially if they feel rejected or if they reject themselves. One lady even shared with me that she felt like a "tourist" at school. However, these children want us to notice that they exist, even though they don't believe much in their own right to existence.

This reminds me of a little girl who hid behind some furniture while her parents were entertaining guests. When they realized she was missing, they all started to look for her, but even though she knew that they were getting more and more worried, she didn't come out of her hiding place. She said to herself: *"I want them to find me. I want them to realize that I exist."* It is so hard for the little girl to believe she has the right to exist that she has to create situations to try to prove that she does.

These children often have bodies that are smaller than average, and so often look like dolls; they look fragile. This is why the mother's reaction is often to overprotect them. They are often told that they're too small for this, too small for that. The children believe what they hear to such an extent that their bodies remain small. For them, being loved amounts to being "smothered." Later on in life their reaction will therefore be to reject or to withdraw when someone loves them, because of their fear of being smothered. Over-protected children feel rejected because they feel they're not accepted for who they are. Because they are so small, others try to think and act for them and instead of feeling loved, the children feel their abilities are being rejected.

Withdrawers don't like to become attached to material things as these could prevent them from withdrawing easily. It's as if they scorned everything material. They wonder what they're doing on this planet and find it hard to believe that they could be happy here. They find everything linked to the spirit, including the intellectual world, more attractive. They don't often use material things for their pleasure as they consider them to be superfluous.

One young lady once told me that she didn't enjoy shopping; she only went to feel alive. *Withdrawers* admit that money is necessary but it doesn't make them happy.

Their detachment from material things creates difficulties for them in their sexual lives. They can come to believe that sexuality interferes with spirituality. Several withdrawn women have told me that they thought sex wasn't spiritual; especially once they were mothers. Many of them even attract a partner who doesn't want to make love to them all through their pregnancy. *Withdrawers* find it difficult to believe that they need sexuality like a normal human being. They attract partners who reject them sexually, or they cut themselves off from their sexuality.

The wound of *rejection* is experienced with the parent of the same sex. If you recognize yourself in the above description, it means that you experienced this *rejection* with your parent of the same sex. This parent was the first person to revive your wound. It is therefore normal and human that you hold a grudge, don't accept, or even hate this parent.

The parent of the same sex teaches us how to love, to love ourselves and to give love. The parent of the opposite sex teaches us how to be loved and how to receive love.

When we don't accept our parent of the same sex, it is normal to decide that we don't want this parent as our model. If you suffer from *rejection*, this non-acceptance of your parent explains the difficulties you have accepting and loving yourself, as you are of the same sex as this parent.

Withdrawers believe they're hopeless, worthless. That's why they will do everything possible to be perfect, so that in their eyes and in the eyes of others, they have a certain worth. The word "hopeless" is often present in their vocabulary when speaking about themselves or others. They will say, for example:

"My boss told me I was hopeless, so I left."

"My mother is hopeless at doing the housework."

"My father has always been hopeless with my mother, just like my husband is with me. I don't blame her for leaving."

A withdrawn man told me during one of my workshops that he felt he was hopeless and good for nothing in the eyes of his father. He said: *"When he speaks to me I feel I'm being crushed and suffocated. I just want to run away because I go to pieces in front of him. I feel oppressed just when he's in the same room as me."* A withdrawn woman told me that when she was 16 her mother told her to disappear and never come back; her mother even said that she could die and that wouldn't bother her. At that moment she decided that her mother was "worthless." To escape from her, she cut herself completely off from her mother from that day on.

It's interesting to see that it's generally the parent of the same sex who encourages the "rejected" child to flee.

One example that comes to mind is that of children who want to leave home and whose parents say: *"Good idea, go, it'll be a weight off our minds."* The children then feel even more rejected and resent that parent even more. This situation arises with parents who are also suffering from *rejection*. They encourage flight because it's something they're familiar with, even though this can be unconscious.

Withdrawers also frequently use the word "non-existent." For example, when asked: *"How's your sex life?"* or *"How's your relationship with such a person?"* withdrawers will reply *non-existent*, whereas most people would simply say that things weren't too good.

They also use the word "disappear." They'll say, for example: *"My father used to call my mum a whore...and I wanted to disappear."* Or *"I wanted my parents to disappear."*

Withdrawers need solitude because they're afraid that they wouldn't know what to do if they received a lot of attention. It's as if their very existence were too much for them. When they're with their family, or with any other group, they stay in the background. They believe that they have to endure unpleasant situations, as if they didn't have the right to decide. They don't see what else they could do. Let's take the example of a little girl who asks her mother to help her with her homework and who is told: *"Can't you see how busy I am? Go and ask your father, he has nothing to do."* Feeling rejected, her first reaction will be to say to herself: *"I'm not lovable enough, that's why my mother doesn't want to help me"* and she'll find somewhere to be alone.

Withdrawers generally have very few friends at school or at work. They are considered to be loners and they are generally left alone. The more they isolate themselves, the more they seem to become invisible. They enter a vicious circle; they wear their masks of *withdrawal* when they feel rejected, so as not to suffer; they become so invisible that others don't see them. They find themselves more and more alone and so feel justified in feeling rejected.

On several occasions, at the end of my workshops when the participants express how the workshop has helped them, I am astounded to notice the presence of someone I haven't seen during the two days of the workshop! My reaction is *"But where was that person all this time?"* Shortly after I realize that these people have the morphology of *withdrawers* and that they managed to be quiet, to ask no questions, and to sit behind others so they couldn't be seen throughout the workshop. When I point out to these people that they were very much in the background, they invariably answer: *"I didn't have anything interesting to say. That's why I didn't speak."*

It's true that *withdrawers* generally speak very little. If they talk a lot, it'll be to try to show off their qualities, and others might judge them as being proud.

Withdrawers often develop skin problems so that they won't be touched. Because the skin is a contact organ, its condition can attract or repel others. Having skin problems is a subconscious way of making sure we won't be touched, especially in the area that is affected. *Withdrawers* have often told me *"I feel that when I'm touched, I'm forced to come out of my cocoon."* When suffering from the wound of *rejection*, people believe that if they live in their own world, they will no longer suffer as they won't reject themselves and others won't reject them. That's why, when in a group, they rarely want to take part and they remain in the background. They disappear into their cocoon.

This is also why *withdrawers* can easily have out - body experiences. Unfortunately they are rarely conscious of this. They can even believe that this phenomenon is normal and that others are often "in a dream," as they are. Their ideas are often scattered, and we sometimes hear them saying, *"I need to pull myself together."* They feel that they're in pieces, especially those whose bodies look like a collection of ill-assorted parts. I've also heard *withdrawers* say: *"I feel cut off from other people. It's as if I weren't there."* Some people have even told me that they had the distinct feeling that there was a separation between the top and bottom halves of their bodies, as if there were a wire tightened around their waists. I knew a woman who had this impression of being separated, but the wire was just under her bust. After using the 'letting go' technique that I teach in one of my workshops, she felt the two parts of her body become one and was extremely surprised at this new sensation. She realized through this that she had not been in her body since childhood. She had never understood what *"having your feet on the ground"* meant.

During my workshops, I've also noticed that many withdrawn women cross their legs under them when sitting on a chair. They would, in fact, prefer to sit on the floor. Not having their feet firmly planted on the ground means they can escape more easily. Paying to attend the workshop shows that part of them wants to be there even though they find it difficult to become integrated. When this happens, I tell them they can choose, either to escape into their own worlds and miss what's going on, or to stay connected and present in what's happening.

As we've said, *withdrawers* feel they were never accepted or welcomed by their parent of the same sex. That doesn't necessarily mean that that parent rejected them. It's just how they felt. If that same soul had come back with a wound of *humiliation* to heal, it would have felt humiliated by the same parent having the same attitude. On the other hand, it's true that *withdrawers* attract more situations where they really are rejected than someone who isn't suffering from the same wound - a brother or sister for example.

People suffering from *rejection* continually seek love from those of the same sex, either from their parent or, by transfer, from others of the same sex. They feel they'll never be complete until they manage to win the love of that parent. They are very sensitive to any comment made by that parent and can easily feel rejected. They develop grudges or even hatred because their suffering is so great. Remember, it takes a great deal of love to be able to hate. Only great love that has been thwarted is transformed into hatred. The wound of *rejection* is so deep that out of the five characters, *withdrawers* will be the most inclined to hate. They can easily go from feeling great love to feeling great hatred. This shows the extent of their inner suffering.

Withdrawers are often worried that they'll reject their parent of the opposite sex. They therefore restrain the words and actions they direct towards this parent, thus they aren't themselves because of their wound. They'll do everything possible not to reject this parent because they don't want to be accused of rejecting anybody. They also want the parent of the same sex to do everything possible so that *they* don't feel rejected. Once again, they can't see that it's their unhealed wound that causes them to feel rejected; it has nothing to do with the parent. If they feel rejected by the parent, or anyone else, they feel responsible and reject themselves thinking that it's their fault.

If you recognize yourself as suffering from the wound of *rejection*, it's really important to accept that even if your parent really rejects you, it's because your wound hasn't healed that you attracted this parent and this situation. If you continue to believe that everything that happens to you is the fault of others, this wound will never heal. The consequences of your reaction to your parents are that you feel more easily rejected by other people of the same sex and you are afraid you might reject people of the opposite sex. If you continue to be afraid that you will reject someone, you'll probably end up doing just that. Remember, the more we feed a fear, the more chance there is of that fear materializing.

The deeper our wound of rejection, the more often we'll attract circumstances where we'll be rejected or where we'll reject someone else.

The more *withdrawers* reject themselves, the more afraid they are of being rejected. They continually put themselves down. They often compare themselves to someone better, and so believe that they aren't as good as others. They can't see that they can be better than others in certain fields. They even find it hard to believe that someone would want them as a friend or as a partner, or that people could really love them. One mother told me that when her children told her they loved her, she could never understand why.

Withdrawers live in ambivalence. When they are chosen, they can't believe it, they reject themselves and sometimes end up sabotaging the situation. When they aren't chosen, they feel rejected. Someone who came from a large family told me that his father never chose him for anything. His deduction was that all the others were better than he. It is therefore not surprising that they were chosen instead. It becomes a vicious circle.

Withdrawers may think that what they say or do is worthless. When they receive a lot of attention, they can fall apart, fearing that they're taking up too much space. If they take up a lot of space, they believe that they bother others. In their eyes, being a bother means that they'll be rejected by the person or people they believe they bother. They will continue to stay in the background as long as their wound hasn't healed.

When *withdrawers* speak and someone interrupts them, their immediate reaction is to think that it's because they aren't important and they usually stop speaking. People who don't suffer from *rejection* wouldn't think that they're not important; they would think that it's what they're *saying* that isn't important. *Withdrawers* also find it hard to give their opinions if they haven't been asked, because they feel that the others will feel confronted and will reject them.

If they need to ask something but the person they need to ask is busy, they won't disturb them. They know what they want but don't dare ask for it, believing that it isn't important enough to warrant bothering others.

Several women have told me that they stopped confiding in their mothers when they were teenagers for fear of not being understood. They equated understanding with love. Being understood has nothing to do with being loved. Loving is accepting the other person even if we don't understand. Because of this belief, *withdrawers* become evasive when they speak. They try to evade the subject at hand and fear speaking about other subjects. They act this way primarily with other women. Don't forget that if it's a withdrawn man, he'll experience the same thing with his father and other men.

Another characteristic of *withdrawers* is that they seek perfection in everything they do, because they believe that if they make a mistake, they'll be judged. For them, being judged equals being rejected. As they don't believe in the perfection of their being, they make up for it by trying to reach perfection in what they *do*. They unfor-

41

tunately confuse "being" with "doing." Their need for perfection can even become an obsession. They so much want everything they "do" to be perfect, that each task takes them longer than necessary. This, of course, attracts other situations where they will be rejected.

Withdrawers' greatest fear is panic. As soon as they think they may panic in a given situation, their instinctive reaction is to run away, to hide or to withdraw. They prefer to disappear because they know that if they panic, they'll be frozen to the spot. They believe that if they run away they'll avoid a calamity. They are so convinced that they wouldn't be able to deal with their panic that they can easily come to believe there's a possibility for future panic, even when it's not the case. Wanting to disappear is innate for *withdrawers*. I've often heard them say, during regressions to the fetal state, that they even tried to hide when they were in their mothers' womb. As you can see, it starts very early.

As we attract the type of situations and people into our lives that frighten us, so *withdrawers* frequently attract situations or people into their lives that make them panic. Their fear makes the situation even more dramatic. However, they find all sorts of ways to justify their *withdrawal*, their escape.

Withdrawers panic and remain frozen to the spot more easily with the parent or others of the same sex (especially if these people remind them of that parent). They don't have the same sort of fear with the parent or people of the opposite sex. They can face them more easily. I've also noticed that *withdrawers* often use the word *panic* in their vocabulary. They'll say, for example: "*I'm panic-stricken at the idea of giving up smoking.*" Another person, not suffering from the wound of *rejection*, would simply have said they found it difficult to stop smoking.

The fear of panicking also makes *withdrawers* lose their memory in certain situations. They believe that they have a memory problem when in fact it's a problem of fear. During the course *Become a Workshop Organizer / Lecturer,* I often notice that when people with *withdrawn* characteristics come to the front to give a talk to the others, their fear becomes so strong that, at the last minute, even if they are well prepared and know the subject, they draw a blank. They sometimes even leave their body completely, in front of us all, frozen to the spot as if they were in a dream. Fortunately, this problem sorts itself out as the *withdrawers* heal their wound of *rejection*.

It is interesting to observe that our wounds also affect the way we eat. Human beings feed their physical body in the same way they feed their emotional and mental bodies. *Withdrawers* prefer small portions and often lose their appetite when they're afraid or when they're going through an emotional time. They are more likely to suffer from anorexia than any of the other types. Anorexics cut themselves off almost completely from food because they think they're too fat when in fact, they're thin. It's their way of trying to disappear. On the occasions they eat greedily, they're actually trying to escape through food. It is, however, rare for *withdrawers* to use food for escape. They more often choose alcohol or drugs.

When they are very frightened, *withdrawers* need sugar. As fear drains us of our energy, we often think that by eating sugar, we'll have more energy. Unfortunately, extra sugar only supplies a short burst of energy after which the need for more sugar arises once again.

Our ego does everything possible to stop us from seeing our wounds. Why? Because unconsciously we've given it permission to do that. We are so afraid of once again going through the pain associated with each wound that we avoid, in every way possible, admitting to ourselves that if we are going through *rejection* it's because we reject ourselves. Those who reject us in our lives are there to show us to what extent we reject ourselves.

Our wounds prevent us from being ourselves; this creates a block and can eventually cause illness. Each wound attracts specific complaints and illnesses depending on our inner attitude.

Here are some complaints and illnesses from which *withdrawers* may suffer:

• They frequently suffer from DIARRHEA because they reject their food before their body has had time to assimilate the nutritive elements, just as they too quickly reject themselves or a situation that could be good for them.

• Others suffer from ARRHYTHMIA, an irregularity of the heartbeat. When their heart begins to race, they have the feeling that it wants to burst through their chest; that it wants to get out. It's another way of escaping a difficult situation.

• I mentioned earlier that the wound of *rejection* hurts so much that it is absolutely normal for *withdrawers* to hate their parent of the same sex, the one they accused when young of making them suffer. They find it very difficult to forgive themselves for having held a grudge against this parent, and so they prefer not to see it or see that they still hold a grudge. If they don't allow themselves to hate their parent of the same sex, they may develop CANCER, an illness associated with resentment or hatred resulting from pain endured in isolation. When these people manage to admit to themselves that they resented their parent, they won't develop cancer. They may create a violent illness if they have thoughts of violence against that parent, but it won't be cancer. Cancer is mainly found in people who have suffered a lot and accuse themselves. They don't want to see that they resented their parent, because admitting their resentment would mean admitting that they're horrible and heartless. It would also mean admitting that they reject that parent, when in fact they accuse that parent of rejecting them. *Withdrawers* never allow themselves to be children. They force themselves to become mature quickly, believing that in this way they will be less vulnerable to *rejection*. That's why their bodies, or parts of them, can look like a child's. Cancer shows that they didn't allow their inner child to suffer. They can't accept that it's absolutely normal to resent the parent they thought responsible for their suffering.

- BREATHING PROBLEMS can also be found among the other complaints and illnesses that affect *withdrawers*, especially when they panic.

- They can also suffer from ALLERGIES that reflect their *rejection* in relation to certain foods or substances.

- They can also choose to VOMIT the food they have just eaten to show their *rejection* of a person or a situation. I've already heard young people saying: *"I would like to vomit my mother (or father)." Withdrawers* can express their desire to "vomit" a person or a situation by saying: *"You make me sick"* or *"that makes me sick."* It's their way of expressing their desire to reject someone or something.

- For *withdrawers*, fainting or suffering from BLACKOUTS are other ways to escape a situation or a person.

- In more serious cases, *withdrawers* use a COMA as a means of escape.

- People suffering from AGORAPHOBIA use this behavior disorder to escape certain people or situations that could make them panic. (See the definition of this behavior disorder on page 67).

- If *withdrawers* eat too much sugar, they can attract illnesses of the pancreas such as HYPOGLYCEMIA or DIABETES.

• If they feel a lot of hatred for a parent because of the pain caused by their perceived *rejection* and they feel that they have reached their emotional and mental limit, *withdrawers* can become DEPRESSIVE or MANIC-DEPRESSIVE. If they think of suicide, they don't talk about it, and if they decide to kill themselves they do everything possible to succeed. Those who often talk about suicide and who fail in their attempts often suffer from *abandonment*. I speak about this in the next chapter.

• Because *withdrawers* find it difficult to recognize themselves as "someone" when they are young, they often try to become someone else: they lose themselves in the personality of someone they admire - for example, the young girl who wants to become Madonna. This will last until the day the young girl decides to become someone else. The danger with this excessive behavior is that later it can develop into PSYCHOSIS.

People battling with the other wounds can also develop the above complaints and illnesses, but these illnesses seem to be much more commonly found in people suffering from *rejection*.

If you recognize that you suffer from the wound of *rejection*, it is more than likely that your parent of the same sex was also rejected by their same-sex parent. Moreover, it is highly probable that your parent also felt rejected by *you*. Even if it is unconscious on both sides, this observation holds true for thousands of *withdrawers*.

You must remember that our inability to forgive ourselves for what we do to ourselves or for what we have done to others is the main reason for the presence of any wound. It's difficult to forgive ourselves because we generally can't even see that we blame ourselves. The greater the wound of *rejection*, the more you reject yourself or other people, situations or projects.

We blame others for everything we do ourselves but don't want to see.

That's why we attract people who show us what we do to others or to ourselves.

Another way to recognize that we reject ourselves or others is to feel shame. Every time we want to hide ourselves or our behavior, it's because we feel ashamed. It's normal to find it shameful that our behavior is the same as the behavior we criticize in others. We really don't want them to find out that we act the same way they do.

Remember, all of this is true only when we suffer from rejection and decide to wear our withdrawer mask, believing that in this way we'll avoid suffering from the depth of our wound.

This mask is sometimes worn for only a few minutes a week, sometimes almost permanently.

The distinctive behavior of *withdrawers* is dictated by the fear of once again experiencing the wound of *rejection*. It is, however, probable that you recognize yourself in some of the attitudes but not in everything I've written.

It is almost impossible for one person to acknowledge all the attitudes and behavior patterns mentioned. Each wound has its own inner behavior and attitudes. The thinking, feeling, speaking and acting that are linked to each wound therefore show a reaction to what's happening in life. People who are reacting are not centered, are not in their hearts and can't be happy. That's why it's so useful to be aware of when we are being ourselves and when we are reacting. When we can recognize the difference, we will become the masters of our lives instead of letting ourselves be controlled by our fears.

The aim of this chapter is to help you become familiar with the wound of *rejection*. If you see yourself in the description of the *withdrawer* mask, the last chapter contains all the information you'll need to heal this wound and to once again become yourself, without believing that the world is filled with *rejection*. If you don't see yourself in this description, I suggest you check with those who know you well to see if they agree with you before eliminating the possibility. I've already mentioned that it is possible to have a relatively small wound of *rejection*. In this case, you might have only a few of the characteristics. Remember that it is important to first go by the physical description because unlike us, the physical body never lies; we can easily lie to ourselves.

If you recognize people around you as suffering from this wound, you mustn't try to change them. Try to use what you learn in this book to develop more compassion, to understand their reactive behavior. It would be better that they read this book themselves if they show an interest, rather than trying to explain the contents in your words.

Characteristics of the wound of REJECTION

The awakening of the wound: From conception to one year old. Don't believe they have the right to exist. With the parent of the same sex.

Mask: Withdrawer

Body: Contracted, narrow, thin or fragmented.

Eyes: Small, fearful or give the impression that there's a mask around the eyes.

Vocabulary: "Hopeless" "Nothing" "Non-existent" "Disappear"

Character: Detached from the material world. Perfectionist. Intellectual. Go from great love to deep hate. Don't believe in their right to exist. Sexual difficulties. Think they are hopeless, worthless. Seek solitude. Withdrawn. Are able to make themselves invisible. Find different ways to withdraw. Can easily have out - body experiences. Feel misunderstood. Find it difficult to let their inner child live.

Greatest fear: panic

Eating habits: appetite spoiled by emotions or fear. Small portions. To escape: sugar, alcohol or drugs. Predisposition to anorexia.

Possible illnesses: Skin problems, diarrhea, arrhythmia, cancer, breathing problems, allergies, vomiting, fainting, coma, hypoglycemia, diabetes, depression, suicidal tendencies, psychosis.

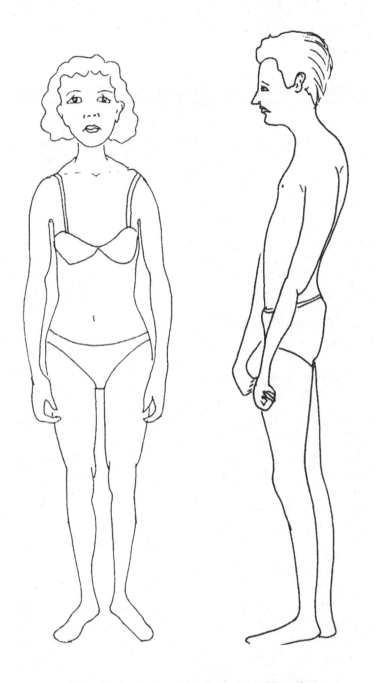

**Body of a person suffering
from the wound of ABANDONMENT
(Dependent mask)**

Chapter 3

Abandonment

To *abandon* someone is to leave, to desert, to no longer want to take care of that person. Many of us confuse *rejection* with *abandonment*. Let's look at the difference using a couple as our example. In a relationship, those who *reject* their partners push them away, no longer wanting them at their sides. Those who *abandon* their partners leave; they go away to distance themselves temporarily or permanently.

The wound inflicted with *abandonment* is more at the level of *having* and *doing* than at the level of *being* as is the case with the wound of *rejection*. Here are some situations that may awaken the wound of *abandonment* in a young child:

Small children may feel abandoned...

... if their mothers are suddenly very busy with a new baby. The feeling of *abandonment* will be even greater if that baby needs more care because of an illness or handicap. Children in this situation feel that their mother is continually leaving (abandoning) them to take care of the baby, and they begin to believe that their relationship with their mother will never be the same.

... if their parents go to work every day and have very little time for them.

... if they are taken to hospital and have to stay. They don't understand what's happening to them, and if they feel they have been the least bit unpleasant prior to arriving at the hospital (and if they think their parents were fed up with them), the feeling of *abandonment* could be even stronger. At the hospital they may decide to believe that their parents have abandoned them forever. Even if their parents visit every day, the pain experienced at the moment they felt abandoned will have the upper hand. This pain prompts them to begin to create a mask, believing this mask will protect them from experiencing the pain again.

... if their parents take them to be looked after for a few days, perhaps during the holidays, even if they are to stay with their grandma while the parents are away.

... if their mother is always ill and their father too busy or absent to look after them so they have to manage by themselves.

I knew a woman who was incredibly frightened when her father died when she was 18. She felt that he had abandoned her. His death had a great impact on her because, for several years, her mother had continually told her that she would have to leave home as soon as she was 21. This woman, who already felt rejected by her mother, was afraid because her only thought was: *"What's going to happen to me when I have to leave home all alone, now that Daddy's not there to look after me?"*

Many people suffering from the wound of *abandonment* have declared that when they were young, their fathers or mothers (the parent of the opposite sex) didn't communicate with them. They found that parent too withdrawn, and often resented them for letting the other parent take up all the space. Many were convinced that their parent just wasn't interested in them.

According to my observations, the wound of *abandonment* is experienced with the parent of the opposite sex. I have, however, noticed that people suffering from *abandonment* often suffer from *rejection* as well. When these children were young, they felt rejected by their parent of the *same* sex and abandoned by the parent of the *opposite* sex who, in their opinion, should have looked after them better, and above all, protected them from the other parent's *rejection*. The example of the woman who lost her father when she was 18 clearly illustrates the double wound of *rejection* and *abandonment*.

Children can feel abandoned by their parent of the same sex but, in fact, it's more likely to be the wound of *rejection* they experience with this parent. Why? Because parents who don't nurture their same-sex children act this way because they reject *themselves,* and that's what their children feel deep down. When parents reject themselves and have a child of the same sex, it's absolutely normal and human to unconsciously reject this child, because she or he constantly reminds them of the selves they have rejected.

As you go deeper into this character study, you'll realize that most people have several wounds. However, all wounds don't carry the same degree of pain.

Those who suffer from *abandonment* don't feel sufficiently nourished with affection. The lack of physical nourishment can also cause the wound of *abandonment*, which generally appears before the age of two. The mask that we create to try to hide this wound from ourselves is the DEPENDENT mask. I will therefore use *dependent* as the word to describe someone who suffers from *abandonment*.

This mask is characterized by a body that lacks muscle tone. A long, slim body that tends to droop shows a deeper wound of *abandonment*. The muscular system is underdeveloped and doesn't seem able to hold the body upright, as if it needed help to stand; the legs are weak. The body expresses exactly what is going on inside the person. *Dependents* believe that they'll never be able to make it alone and that they need someone to lean on. In this person, we can easily see the little child who needs help.

Big, sad eyes also indicate a wound of *abandonment*, eyes that seem to want to draw other people to them. We often have the impression that the *dependent's* arms are too long, that they hang too close to the body. These are people who don't seem to know what to do with their arms when they're standing up, especially when others are looking at them. Another characteristic of the *dependent* mask is that some parts of the body, such as the shoulders, bust, buttocks, cheeks, stomach, scrotum for men, etc.

hang, or are flabby. Some parts might be lower than normal. Their backs may also be rounded, as if the spine can't completely support them.

As you can see, the *dependent's* most striking physical characteristic is the lack of flesh tone. When we see a part of the body that droops, we can assume that person is wearing the *dependent* mask to hide a wound of *abandonment*.

Don't forget that the size of the mask is relative to the depth of the wound. A very dependent person will have all of the above characteristics. If you see only a few, the wound is not so deep. It's important to know that if a person is both fat and lacking muscle tone in parts of the body, the lack of tone indicates the wound of *abandonment*, whereas the excess weight indicates a different wound that we'll see later in the book.

It is important to learn to see the difference between the *withdrawer* mask (the wound of *rejection*) and the *dependent* mask. There may be two very slim people next to you; one is withdrawn and the other dependent. Both may have small ankles and wrists. The difference mainly lies in their tone. *Withdrawers* will stand straight despite the fact that they're slim or small, whereas the posture of the *dependent* will be more slumped. We also have the impression that *withdrawers'* skin is stuck to their bones but that underneath there is a solid muscular system, whereas *dependents* have more skin but less tone. We may find some physical characteristics of the *withdrawer* and some physical characteristics of the *dependent* in someone who suffers both from the wound of *rejection* and the wound of *abandonment.* The wound that is the most obvious is the one causing the most suffering.

Because the body tells everything about ourselves, more and more of us try to change our physical appearance through plastic surgery or overdeveloping our muscles through weight lifting. When we try to hide our body from others, it means we're trying to hide the wounds that correspond to the altered parts.

The only way to discover these altered parts in others is to use our intuition. Once, while observing a woman during a consultation, I noticed she had a nice firm bust; however, my first impression had been that her bust sagged. It was just a "flash" of intuition. As I have learned to trust my intuition, I said: *"It's strange, I can see that you have a nice firm bust, but when I first saw you I could have sworn that your bust sagged. Did you by any chance have an operation?"* She confirmed that she had undergone plastic surgery because she didn't like her breasts.

Some details, like flesh tone, are harder to see in a woman than in a man because a woman's bra, shoulder pads, and other accessories can mislead us. In any case, if you look in the mirror you can't lie to yourself. I therefore recommend that you follow your intuition and go with your first impression when observing another person.

I know men who have been lifting weights for years and yet, in spite of their big beautiful muscles, we can sense a lack of tone. That explains why, when these men stop working out, they end up with a flabby body. This occurs only in dependent men. We cannot heal a wound by hiding it. Let me come back to my example of the wounded hand, mentioned in the first chapter. We can hide our wound in a glove or a bandage, that doesn't mean that it's healed.

Out of the five types mentioned in this book, *dependents* are most apt to become victims. There's a strong possibility that one or even both of their parents are also victims. Victims often create all types of problems in their lives, especially physical problems, to attract attention. This meets the *dependent's* need for attention - they can never get enough of it. When it seems they're doing everything possible to attract attention, they are in fact trying to feel important enough to receive support. They believe that if they don't manage to get another's attention, they'll never be able to count on that person. This phenomenon can be seen in *dependents* when they are very young. *dependent* children need to feel that if they stumble, they'll be able to count on someone to set them back on their feet.

Dependents often blow things out of proportion; the slightest incident becomes a major problem. If, for example, their partner doesn't phone to say they'll be late, a *dependent* will think the worst and won't understand why their partner made them suffer so much when they could have phoned. When we see a person behaving like a victim, we often wonder how they manage to attract so many problems. *Dependents* don't see these events as problems because through their problems they receive attention, and for them, that's a big gift. They therefore don't feel abandoned, and being abandoned is more painful for them than all the problems they attract. Only other *dependents* can really understand that. The more they act the victim, the deeper their wound of *abandonment*.

I've noticed that very often victims like to play the role of savior. For example, *dependents* will play the role of parent with their brothers and sisters or will try to save someone they love who is in a difficult situation. These are subtle means to receive attention. On the other hand, when *dependents* do a lot for someone else, it's because they want to be complimented, to feel important. These people often end up with backache, because they carry responsibilities that don't belong to them.

Dependents most need the support of others. Whether or not they find it difficult to make decisions by themselves, *dependents* will generally ask for the opinion or the approval of others before deciding. They need to feel supported in their decisions. That's why they often appear to find it difficult to make decisions, but in fact they only have problems making up their minds when they don't feel backed up by others. Their expectations from others are relative to what the others can do for them. They are not, however, necessarily seeking physical help; they just need to feel supported by someone in what they're doing or in what they want to do. When they feel supported, they feel loved. It is true that, in general, they don't like activities or physical work that must be done alone; they need the presence of someone else to support them.

Although they need support, it's interesting to note that *dependents* often use the expression "*I can't stand...*" This shows to what extent we do to others, without realizing it, what we accuse them of doing or what we fear they'll do to us.

When *dependents* do something for someone else, they expect affection in return. When they receive the desired affection while doing something pleasant with that person, they want it to last. When it ends they'll say: *"What a pity that it's already over."* The end of something pleasant is experienced, of course, as *abandonment*.

dependent women who are in their victim role will have a small childlike voice and ask a lot of questions. We can see that they have great difficulty accepting refusal when they ask for help, and they tend to insist. The more they suffer when someone says no, the more they'll be prepared to use everything in their power to obtain what they want; manipulation, sulking, or even blackmail.

Dependents often ask for advice because they don't feel able to manage alone (but they don't necessarily follow the advice they receive). They'll end up doing what they want because they weren't really seeking help, just support. When walking, they often let others go in front because they're happier when others are guiding them. They believe that if they manage too well on their own, nobody will take care of them in the future, which will result in the isolation they're seeking so desperately to avoid.

Dependents often have ups and downs. For a while, they are happy and everything's fine, then suddenly, they feel unhappy and sad. They even wonder why - because very often, there's no apparent reason for this change in mood. If they looked closely, they would probably discover their fear of solitude.

Solitude is the greatest fear for *dependents*. They're convinced that they'll never be able to deal with solitude. That's why they hang on to others and do everything possible to receive attention. They're prepared to do whatever it takes to be loved, so they won't be deserted. Their fear is: "*What will I do all by myself? What will become of me? What will happen to me?*" They are often in turmoil because, on the one hand, they ask for a lot of attention and on the other hand, they fear that if they ask for too much, the other will get fed up and leave them. Though they may not admit it, *dependents* will put up with, and willingly suffer from, situations that others would find intolerable. Let's take the example of a woman who lives with an alcoholic or an abusive partner. She fears that her suffering might be even greater if she leaves her partner than it is when she's with him. In fact, she lives in hope, emotional hope. She can't admit her wound, because if she did, she might go through the suffering that this wound represents.

Dependent people are the most able to remain oblivious to problems in their relationship. They prefer to believe that everything's fine because they fear they'll be abandoned. If their partners say they want to leave, *dependents* suffer tremendously because, having been oblivious to their problems, they didn't expect that decision. If this is your case, if you see yourself hanging on, doing everything possible to avoid *abandonment*, you have to give *yourself* support. Find a mental image; imagine something that supports you. Above all, don't let yourself down when you're going through moments of despair and you believe that you can no longer receive support from outside. You may believe that you can't manage alone, but there is a solution to every problem. If you support yourself, things will become clearer and you'll find the solution.

Dependents have great problems with the word "leave" which they associate with the word "abandonment." If for example, *dependents* are with someone who says: *"I have to leave you now, I have to go,"* they feel hurt. Just hearing the word *leave,* even if it's on the phone, causes suffering. The other person would have to explain their reason for going without using the word *leave,* for the *dependent* not to feel abandoned. When they feel abandoned, they feel they're not important enough to deserve attention from others. I've often noticed that, when I'm with *dependents*, if I dare look at my watch to check the time (something that I often do because of my full schedule) their expression changes. I feel how strongly this gesture affects them. They immediately believe that what I have to do is more important than they are.

These people also find it difficult to leave a situation or a place. Even if the place they're going to seems nice, the idea of leaving makes them sad. Let's take the example of going on a trip for a few weeks. They'll find it hard to leave their loved ones, their job or their home. Once they reach their destination, and the time comes for them to leave that place and the people there, they'll once again find it hard.

The most intense emotion that *dependents* feel is sadness. They feel this sadness deep inside and are unable to understand or explain where it comes from. They seek the presence of others to avoid feeling this sadness. They can, however, go to the other extreme, and withdraw from or leave the person or the situation that makes them feel sad or lonely. They don't realize that each time they leave someone or something, they in turn are abandoning. When going through a crisis, they can even think of suicide. In general, they will only talk about it or threaten to do it, but they won't act because all they're looking for is support. If they do attempt to kill themselves, they'll usually fail. If however, after several attempts, nobody wants to support them, they really could commit suicide.

Dependents are also frightened of all forms of authority. They imagine that someone who looks or sounds authoritarian wouldn't want to take care of them. They find authoritarians indifferent and cold. That's why *dependents* are warm to others, even if they have to force themselves. They believe that in this way others will be warm and attentive, not cold and authoritarian.

Dependents often use the word *absent* or *alone*. When speaking of their childhood for example, they'll say that they were often left alone, that their mother or father was absent. A sign that they suffer from isolation is that they feel great anxiety at the idea of being alone. A person can feel alone, but without suffering. A *dependent* may feel that everything would be so much better if they had someone else with them. Their degree of anxiety determines the degree of suffering. Feeling isolated also generates a feeling of emergency in these people because they fear that what they lack will be refused or inaccessible or unavailable at the moment they most need it. Hiding behind the feeling of isolation is the fact that the people who suffer from this unconsciously shut themselves off from the thing or the person they so desire to have near them. They don't open themselves up to receive or accept the desired thing or person because they fear they wouldn't be able to deal with it. They also fear that receiving all that attention might make them experience emotions that are too heavy for them. This behavior can easily be seen in all people who sabotage their own happiness. As soon as a relationship becomes more intense, they find a way of making it come to an end.

Dependent people cry easily, especially when talking about their problems or their ordeals. Their tears show us how they accuse others of letting them down when all their problems and illnesses arise. They even accuse GOD of abandoning them, and feel they have good reason to do so. They don't realize that often, they also let other people down. They don't realize how many half-finished projects they abandon. Their ego once again manages to trick them (like all our egos do).

Dependents need the attention and presence of others but they don't realize how many times they don't do to others what they want others to do to them. They would like, for example, to sit down alone and read a book, but they wouldn't want their partner to do the same thing. They like going to certain places alone when they choose to, but they would feel abandoned and deserted if their partner did the same. They would think: *"That's it, I'm not important enough to be taken."* It's also difficult for *de-*

pendents when they're not invited to a meeting or a get-together when, logically, they feel they should have been. They feel incredibly sad, abandoned and unimportant.

Dependents physically hang on to their loved ones. When young, the little girl will hang on to her father and the little boy to his mother. When in a couple, *dependents* lean on their partner or touch or frequently hold hands. When standing up, they lean against a wall, a door or anything else. Even when they're sitting, they find it difficult to stay upright; they lean on the arm of the chair or they lounge. In all cases, they find it hard to stand straight, and their backs often hunch forward.

When you see someone who seeks a lot of attention in a public meeting, look at that person's body and you'll see the *dependent*. During my workshops there are always people who come to see me during the breaks and before and after the course starts to ask me questions in private. Without fail, these people are wearing their *dependent* masks. Most of the time I ask them to ask their questions during the course because they are good questions and the answers could interest the other participants. When the workshop starts up again, they often fail to ask their questions. What interested them was the attention I could have given them in private. I sometimes advise these people to follow a private therapy where they'll be able to obtain all the attention they want. This solution does, however, have its limits, because it could feed the wound rather than heal it.

Another way to attract attention is to have a public position with a large audience. Many singers, actors, comedians and others working in the artistic field with a large public following, are *dependents*. They feel good in any role where they are the stars.

In private consultations, *dependents* are the most likely to transfer onto their therapists. They are in fact looking to the therapist for the support they never received from a parent or a partner. A friend of mine who is a psychologist once told me that one of her patients had a fit of jealousy when she told him that she would be replaced by a colleague during her two-week vacation with her husband. That was how she realized that the patient had transferred onto her. We checked and realized that he was a *dependent*. I'll take advantage of this example to warn all those who work in counseling to be particularly aware of the risk of transference when working with someone suffering from *abandonment*.

Dependents bond easily with others, which makes them feel responsible for the happiness and sadness of others, just as they feel that others are responsible for their happiness or sadness. People who need to bond are too sympathetic. They feel other peoples' emotions easily and are easily overwhelmed. Their desire to bond is at the root of many fears that can even lead to agoraphobia. Here is my definition of AGORAPHOBIA as described in my book *Your Body Says: Love Yourself!*

This phobia is a pathological fear of open spaces and public places. It is the most common of all phobias. Women are twice as sensitive to this phobia as men. Many men drown their agoraphobia in alcohol. They would rather become alcoholics than admit their great uncontrollable fear. Agoraphobics often complain that they suffer from anxiety and, above all, anguish, to the point of panicking. Agoraphobics will have physiological reactions (palpitations, blackouts, muscular tension or weakness, perspiration, breathing problems, incontinence, nausea, etc.) in stressful situations, which can lead to panic; cognitive reactions (feeling strange, fear of losing control, of going mad, of being publicly humiliated, of fainting or of dying, etc.) and behavioral reactions (fleeing anxiety causing situations and naturally, any place that seems to be at a distance from the place or the person that makes them feel secure. Most agoraphobics suffer from hypoglycemia.

The fear and the sensations that agoraphobics feel are so strong that they avoid situations they wouldn't be able to flee. That's why agoraphobics must find someone they're close to, who becomes the person they feel secure with when they go out, and a place they feel safe in, where they can hide. Some even stop going out all together. They always find a good reason. In fact, the catastrophes they anticipate never occur. Most agoraphobics were very dependent on their mothers when young and felt responsible for their happiness, or helped them as mothers. Agoraphobics can help themselves emotionally by solving their situations with their mothers.

The two great fears that haunt agoraphobics are: the fear of death and the fear of madness. Having met agoraphobics in nearly all the workshops I've given over the years, I was able to draw up an interesting synthesis concerning agoraphobia and this synthesis has helped hundreds of agoraphobics. Their fears stem from childhood and they are fears that were experienced in isolation. Death or insanity among close ones are circumstances that favor the development of agoraphobia. It's also possible that the agoraphobic nearly died when young or that the fear of death or insanity was brought into the family from outside.

Agoraphobics at all levels feel this fear of death, even though they aren't really aware of this. They don't feel able to face up to change at any level because for them, change is a symbolic death. That's why they feel great anguish and their degree of agoraphobia is accentuated when going through change. These changes can be the passage from childhood to adolescence, from adolescence to adulthood, from being single to being married, a move, a separation, a change in job, a pregnancy, an accident, death or birth.

For several years these fears and anguish can be unconscious and contained. Then one day, when the agoraphobics have reached their mental and emotional limits, they can no longer contain themselves and their fears become conscious and apparent.

Agoraphobics also have uncontrollable, vivid imaginations. They imagine situations that are way beyond reality, and feel unable to face these changes. They fear insanity because of their intense mental activity. They don't dare speak to others about this, as they don't want to be judged as being mad. It's crucial to realize that it isn't *madness, just sensitivity that's too acute and not well integrated.*

If you recognize yourself in the above description, you must realize that what you're going through isn't insanity and you can't die from it. You were just too open to other peoples' emotions when you were young, and you felt responsible for their happiness or unhappiness. You have however, become very psychic and are able to foresee other peoples' misfortunes. That's why you pick up other peoples' emotions and fears when you are in a public place. You really need to learn the real notion of responsibility. The notion you have believed in so far is no good for you. This notion of responsibility is part of the teachings of Listen to Your Body.

I've noticed that most of the agoraphobics that I've met up to now are *dependents*. If you refer to the definition of agoraphobia, you'll see that the fear of insanity and death is mentioned. When someone dear to a *dependent* dies, they feel abandoned. They find it more and more difficult to accept death, because each death awakens their wound of *abandonment* and accentuates their degree of agoraphobia. People who have a predominating wound of *abandonment* are more frightened by death, whereas those who have a predominating wound of *betrayal* are more frightened by the idea of going mad. We will address the wound of *betrayal* in the fifth chapter.

Dependent mothers need to bond, and depend a great deal on the love they receive from their children. They'll do everything possible to let their children know how much they mean to them. Love from others, especially from those they are close to, provides *dependents* with a lot of support. It helps them stand on their own two feet. I've often heard *dependents* say: "*I can't bear to feel that somebody doesn't like or love me; I'll do anything and everything to change that.*" When *dependents* say: "*Please call me to tell me how you're doing,*" they are in fact saying: "*When you call, I feel important.*" They need others, at all costs, in order to feel they're being taken into consideration and are important; they can't manage by themselves.

When *dependents* come into contact with the problems their dependency generates, they then wish to become independent. It's very common for *dependents* to believe that they're independent and they enjoy telling others how independent they are. This, however, only hides the wound of *abandonment* and accentuates it all the more because it isn't being healed.

Dependent men or women can, for example, decide they don't want children because they want to keep their independence. This decision, on the part of a man, often hides the fear that he won't receive all the attention from his partner if there is a child in the home. A *dependent* woman would be more likely to worry about feeling suffocated by the obligations that go with having a child. If, on the other hand, she does want children, she'll prefer the moments when they're young and heavily *dependent* on her. That makes her feel more important. *Dependents* should seek autonomy rather than independence. I explain this further in the last chapter.

Dependents exhibit the same behavior in their sex life. They often use sex to draw the other person. This is especially noticeable in women. When *dependents* feel desired by others, they feel more important. Of the five types, I'd say that the person who most fears being abandoned is the one who most likes sex. They often want more sex than their partners, and it's not infrequent to see that those who complain of the lack of sex are those who suffer from the wound of *abandonment* and wear the *dependent* mask.

If a *dependent* woman doesn't want to make love, she won't tell her partner. She prefers to pretend because she doesn't want to miss out on an opportunity to feel desired. I've even known women who accepted to live in a threesome, knowing that their husband was making love to another woman in the other room. *Dependent* men, on the other hand, will pretend they don't know their wife has a lover. *Dependents* will choose to endure difficult situations of this type rather than be abandoned. It's not what they prefer, but they're prepared to do anything to keep their partner.

Concerning food, *dependents* can eat a lot without putting on weight. As their general inner attitude is that they never have enough, this is also the message their bodies receive when they eat. Their bodies therefore react accordingly. When people eat, even a little, thinking that they're once again eating too much, their bodies receive that message and react as if there was too much food. These people will put on weight.

In the last chapter, I mentioned that *withdrawers* tend to become anorexic whereas *dependents* are more inclined to suffer from bulimia. My observations lead me to conclude that when a *dependent* man is bulimic, it's because he's trying to nourish himself with his mother, as he misses her so much. When a *dependent* woman is bulimic, it's because she misses her father. When these people don't have a substitute for the missing parent, they transfer onto food. The word *eat* is omnipresent in their language. They'll say for example: *"My child eats up all my energy."* or *"My job eats up all my time."*

Dependents prefer soft foods to hard foods. They generally like bread, which is the symbol of the nourishing earth. They'll eat slowly to make the pleasure and the attention last, especially when they are in the company of others. Moreover, *dependents* don't like eating alone, especially when they're out. On top of that, as they have a problem with the word *leave*, they won't want to leave anything on their plates. All this is, of course, unconscious.

Concerning illness, *dependents* are well known for having been frequently ill, weak and puny when young. Here are illnesses that *dependents* are prone to:

- ASTHMA, an illness where expiring is difficult and tiresome. On the metaphysical level, this illness indicates that the person takes more than necessary and has great difficulties giving back.

- *Dependents* also suffer from BRONCHIAL problems as the bronchial tubes have a metaphysical link with the family. When *dependents* have bronchial problems, this shows that they feel they don't receive enough from their families, that they're too dependent on their families. They'd be better off believing they have their place in their family rather than going to extremes to prove it to themselves.

• *Dependents* attract problems in the PANCREAS (hypoglycemia and diabetes) as well as problems in their ADRENAL GLANDS because they bond too easily with others. Their whole digestive system is fragile because they don't feel that they're adequately nourished. Even though this lack of nourishment is not on the physical plane, but is rather situated on an affective level, their physical body, being the reflection of their psyches, receives the message that there's a lack.

• *Dependents* also frequently suffer from MYOPIA. Myopia represents the difficulty in seeing far which is linked to a fear of the future and especially of facing the future alone.

• *Dependents* who are victims can suffer from HYSTERIA. It is said, in psychology, that hysterics are like children who fear being deprived of their mothers' milk and abandoned. That's why they display their emotions noisily.

• Many *dependents* suffer from DEPRESSION when their wounds hurt too much and they feel that they'll never be loved the way they want to be. It's also a way of getting attention.

- *Dependents* suffer from MIGRAINES because they stop themselves from being who they are; they block their "I am." They do too much to try and be what others would like them to be or they live too much in the shadow of the people they love.

- I've also noticed that *dependents* can develop RARE DISEASES or so-called INCURABLE DISEASES, which necessitate particular attention. (I would like to remind you that when medicine qualifies a disease as *incurable*, it is in fact announcing that THEY haven't found a cure YET.)

The above complaints and illnesses can also occur in people suffering from other wounds but they seem to be much more common in people suffering from *abandonment*.

If you recognize yourself as suffering from the wound of *abandonment*, I would like to remind you that this wound is reactivated by your parent of the opposite sex and continues to be reactivated by any other person of the opposite sex. It is therefore absolutely normal and humane to resent that parent or those people. I'll repeat here what I say in most of my books:

As long as we continue resenting a parent (even if it's unconsciously), our relationships with other people of the same sex as that parent will be difficult.

I suggest you check and you'll discover that your parent suffered from the same wound with his or her parent of the opposite sex, in other words, with the parent of your sex. The same wounds are repeated from generation to generation (which also explains the phenomenon of heredity) and this will last as long as we don't stop the wheel of karma. The only way to do that is through real love.

Remember, the main cause of a wound is the inability to forgive ourselves for what we do to ourselves or to others. It's difficult to forgive ourselves because, generally, we can't even see our own self-resentment. The deeper the wound of *abandonment*, the more we abandon ourselves (in other words: we let ourselves down) or we abandon other people, situations or projects. We blame others for everything we do ourselves but don't want to see. That's why we attract people around us who show us what we do to others or to ourselves.

Another way we realize that we abandon others or ourselves is to feel shame. Every time we want to hide our behavior or ourselves, it's because we feel ashamed. It's normal to find it shameful that our behavior is the same as the behavior we criticize in others. We really don't want others to find out that we act in the same way they do.

It is therefore important and urgent to solve everything with our parents, because that's how we'll stop reproducing the same situations. Even medical and psychological scientists have noticed and admitted the perpetuation of certain destructive behaviors or illnesses from generation to generation. They have recognized that there are families of diabetics, heart patients, cancer pa-

tients, asthmatics and also families that are violent, incestuous, alcoholic, etc.

If you recognize the characteristics of the *dependent*
in you, even though you don't feel that you lacked attention from your parent of the opposite sex and on the contrary, you feel that you received a lot, this is what may
have happened: the attention you received may not have
corresponded to the attention you would have liked to receive. You may even have felt suffocated by that attention.

I can offer the example of my eldest son, whose adult
body shows the wound of *abandonment*. He received
more of my attention than the other two when young, because I didn't work outside the house, I was at home with
him. On the other hand, I was too rigid and strict with him
in situations that, according to him, didn't justify that attitude. I never left him alone; I watched over everything he
did because I would have liked to make a perfect human
being out of him, according to my notion of perfection. I
understand today that that wasn't at all the type of attention he wished for. He therefore experienced the wound of
abandonment, and I find it normal that he resented me
when young. I realize today that this experience was part
of his life path and that we had to understand these things
together. He needed a mother like me to be able to go
through his forgiveness process concerning *abandonment*
and I needed a son like him to help me complete things
with my father. I'll speak about that more in the chapter on
betrayal.

Remember, the characteristics and the behavior described in this chapter are only present when people suffering from abandonment decide to wear their dependent mask, believing that in this way they'll avoid suffering from abandonment. Depending on the depth of the wound and the intensity of the pain, this mask can be worn very little or very often.

The distinctive behavior of *dependents* is dictated by the fear of once again experiencing the wound of *abandonment*. It is probable that you recognize yourself in some of the attitudes, but not in everything I've written. It is almost impossible for one person to acknowledge all the attitudes and behavior patterns mentioned. Each wound has its respective inner behavior and attitudes. The thinking, feeling, speaking and acting that are linked to each wound, therefore, show a reaction to what's happening in life. People who are reacting through their masks are not centered in their hearts and can't be happy. That's why it's so useful to be aware of those times when you are being yourself and those times when you are reacting. Through this awareness, you become master of your life rather than letting yourself be controlled by your fears.

This chapter is intended to help you become familiar with the wound of *abandonment*. If you see yourself in the description of the *dependent* mask, the last chapter contains all the information you'll need to heal this wound and to once again become yourself, without believing that the world is filled with *abandonment*. If you don't see yourself in this description, I suggest you check with those who know you well to see if they agree with you.

I've already mentioned that it is possible to have a relatively small wound of *abandonment*. In this case, you might have only a few of the characteristics. Remember that it is important to refer to the physical description first because, though we can easily lie to ourselves, the physical body never lies.

If you recognize people around you as suffering from this wound, you mustn't try to change them. Try to use what you learn in this book to develop more compassion for them, to understand their reactive behavior. It would be better that they read this book themselves if they show an interest, rather than trying to explain the contents in your words.

Characteristics of the wound of
ABANDONMENT

Awakening of the wound: Between one and three years old with the parent of the opposite sex. Lack of affection or of the desired type of affection.

Mask: Dependent

Body: Long, thin, lack of tone, sagging, weak legs, rounded back, arms seem too long and hang close to the body, parts of the body that hang or are flabby.

Eyes: Big, sad. A look that draws.

Vocabulary: "absent" "alone" "I can't stand…" "I'm being eaten"

Character: Victim; need to bond. Need presence, attention, and above all support. Have difficulty doing or deciding alone. Ask for advice they don't necessarily follow. Childlike voice. Difficulties accepting when people say no. Sadness. Cry easily. Attract pity. One day happy, one day sad. Physically hang on to others. Psychic. Star. Seek independence. Like sex.

Greatest fear: Solitude

Eating habits: Good appetite. Bulimic. Like soft foods. Eat slowly.

Possible illnesses: Back, asthma, bronchitis, migraines, hypoglycemia, agoraphobia, diabetes, adrenal glands, myopia, hysteria, depression, rare and incurable diseases that attract attention.

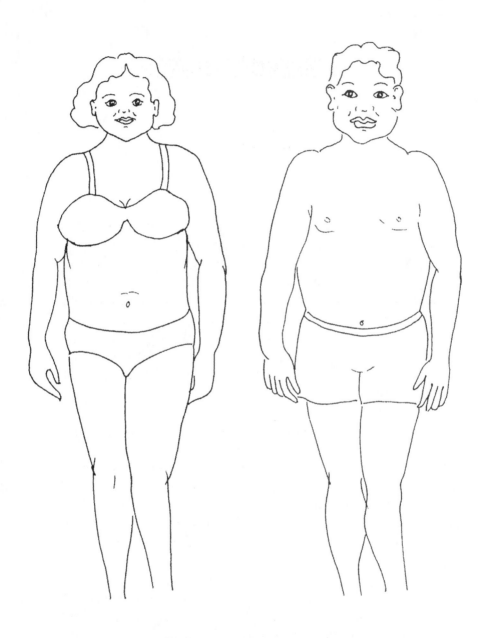

**Body of a person suffering
from the wound of HUMILIATION
(Masochist mask)**

Chapter 4

Humiliation

Let's look at the word "humiliation." Humiliation is defined as the lowering of one's pride, dignity, or self-respect. Synonyms for this word are: "embarrassment," "mortification," "shame," "indignity," "degradation," "abasement." This wound can be awakened between the ages of one and three. I speak of awakening because, as I've already mentioned, it is my theory that when we are born, we have already decided which wounds we want to heal, even though we're not aware of this after our birth.

The soul that comes to heal the wound of *humiliation* will attract one or both parents to humiliate it. This wound is especially linked to the material world, the world of *having* and *doing*. It is awakened while the functions of the physical body are developing, when most children learn to feed themselves, keep themselves clean, go to the toilet alone, speak, listen and understand what adults are saying to them.

The wound is awakened when a child feels that one of his parents is ashamed of him, or he fears they will be ashamed of him if he is dirty, if he makes a mess (especially in public or with family) or if he is badly dressed, etc. Whatever the circumstance that leads the child to feel degraded, compared, mortified, or ashamed at the physical level, it awakens the wound and it starts to grow. Let's take the example of a baby who plays with her "pooh" and gets it all over her bed, or who makes some other sort of "disgusting" mess. The wound will be awakened when she hears her mother telling her father what happened. Even when very young, a baby can feel the parents' disgust, and so can feel humiliated and ashamed.

I remember one case in particular when I was a boarder in a convent. I was six years old. We all used to sleep together in a large dormitory, and when a little girl wet her bed, the nun made her go into all the classes the next day with her stained sheet on her back. The nun thought that by humiliating and mortifying her, it wouldn't happen again. We all know, however, that this type of *humiliation* only makes the situation worse. The wound of a child suffering from *humiliation* will only get bigger through this type of ordeal.

The area of sexuality also contains its fair share of potential *humiliation*. For example, when a mother finds her little boy masturbating and exclaims: *"Aren't you ashamed of yourself? You shouldn't be doing that!"* the child is mortified, feels ashamed and may later have difficulties with his sexuality. If children happen to see one of their parents naked and feel that that parent is ill at ease and wants to hide, they'll learn that you should be ashamed of your body.

The wound of *humiliation* can therefore be activated in different fields depending on what has happened between the ages of one and three. Children feel put down if they feel a parent is controlling them, if they feel they have no freedom to act or move as they would like on a physical level. For example, a child is punished for playing in the mud in his clean clothes just before guests arrive. If the parents then tell the guests about this in front of the child, the child's humiliation will be all the worse. This treatment can lead children to believe that they disgust their parents. They then feel humiliated and ashamed of their behavior. On the other hand, we often hear people suffering from this wound talking about all the forbidden things they did when they were young. It's as if they were looking for situations that would embarrass or humiliate them.

Unlike the four other wounds, which are experienced with a specific parent or with the person who played the role of that parent, the wound of *humiliation* is most often experienced with the mother. It can, however, be experienced with the father if he is the one in control and who plays the role of mother, showing the child how eat properly, stay clean etc. The wound of *humiliation* may also be linked to the mother in the areas of sexuality and cleanliness, and to the father in the areas of learning, listening and speaking. In this case, the wound will have to be healed with both parents.

Children who experience *humiliation* will create the MASOCHIST mask. Masochism is described as gaining satisfaction and even pleasure from suffering. Most of the time *masochists* are not aware that they seek pain and *humiliation*. They manage to punish themselves before someone else does it for them. Even though I've said that the *humiliation* or the shame a *masochist* will experience is mainly in the fields of *having* or *doing*, they can go to great lengths to try to be as others would want them to be. However, it's what they *do* or *don't do* that will trigger their wound of *humiliation*. I've also noticed that *doing* and *having* things become ways to compensate the wound.

From now on, when I use the term *masochist*, I'll be referring to someone who suffers from the wound of *humiliation* and who wears the *masochist* mask to avoid suffering and feeling the pain associated with *humiliation*.

Of course we can go through a shameful or humiliating experience without awakening the wound of *humiliation*. On the other hand, a *masochist* can go through an experience of *rejection* and feel humiliated rather than rejected. It's true that all of the five types in this character study feel shame at one time or another. They are especially ashamed when they are caught red-handed doing to others what they most fear others will do to them. It does seem, however, that the person suffering from the wound of *humiliation* feels shame more often than others.

Let's take a moment to explain the difference between shame and guilt. We feel guilty when we judge that what we have or haven't *done* was bad. When we consider that *we* were bad in doing what we did, we feel shame. The opposite of shame is pride. When we aren't proud of ourselves, we are ashamed; we accuse ourselves and tend to want to hide. We can feel guilty without being ashamed, but we can't feel ashamed without also feeling guilty.

Those wearing the *masochist* mask often consider themselves to be "pigs" - unclean, heartless, or beneath others, so they frequently develop a fat body that they're ashamed of. A fat body is different from a muscular body. A person can weigh twenty kilos more than their "normal" weight and not be fat. They rather seem to be strongly built. *Masochists*, on the other hand, are corpulent due to a surplus of fat. Their bodies are rounded; they seem to be as thick, front to back, as they are wide. We can see that they are round, even if we're looking at them from behind. Strongly built people are more muscular; their bodies are wider than they are thick, and seen from the back they don't appear to be fat. This description applies to both men and women.

The following characteristics can be associated with the *masochist* mask: a short waist, a fat rounded neck, and tension in the neck, throat, jaw and pelvis. The face is often very round and the eyes are open wide and innocent, like those of a child. Many parts of the body are round and chubby: fingers, legs, upper arms, etc. It goes without saying that someone who has all these physical characteristics suffers from a deep wound. If only one part of the body is fat and round - the stomach, the buttocks or the bust, for example - it shows a lesser wound of *humiliation*.

I've noticed that this wound seems to be the most difficult to recognize. I have personally worked with hundreds of *masochists*, especially women, who had an obvious wound of *humiliation*. It took many of them up to a year to admit they were ashamed or felt humiliated. If you recognize the physical characteristics of the *masochist* in your body and you find it hard to see your wound of *humiliation*, don't be surprised. Allow yourself as much time as necessary for the wound to come to the surface. In fact, one of the characteristics of the *masochist* is a dislike of moving too fast. It's even difficult for them to move quickly when they have to, and they feel ashamed when they can't go as fast as others, when walking, for example. They have to learn to allow themselves to go at their own speed.

It is, moreover, difficult to recognize the *masochist* mask in some people because they manage to control their weight well. If you put on weight easily and become round when you're not controlling your diet, you may have this wound, but it may be hidden for the moment. The *rigidity* that enables you to do this is explained in chapter six of this book.

Masochists want to show themselves to be solid and in control, so become very capable and are likely to take on a great deal. That's why they create a large back for themselves so that they can carry more. Let's take the example of a woman who, because she wants to please her husband, allows her mother-in-law to come and live with them. Shortly after, her mother-in-law falls ill and she then feels she has to look after her. *Masochists* have a knack for putting themselves into situations where they have to look after others; that way they can forget themselves even more. The more they take on, the more they put on weight.

Each time *masochists* seem to want to do things for others, they are in fact creating constraints and obligations for themselves. They feel they won't make others ashamed of them while they're helping them, but very often they feel humiliated at letting others take advantage of them. They are also rarely appreciated for what they do. I've heard several *masochist* women say they're fed up with being a *slave.* They complain but continue to act in the same way because they don't realize that they create their own constraints. I've also heard several expressions such as: *"After 30 years of loyal service, the management threw me out just like you throw out rubbish!!!"* People like this, who consider themselves to be devoted, really don't feel appreciated. It is, moreover, interesting to note the *humiliation* experienced in such an expression. A *non-masochist* would simply have said: *"After 30 years of service, they dismissed me."* without using such a word as rubbish.

Masochists don't realize that by doing everything for others, they make others feel they couldn't manage alone, thus humiliating *them.* Some *masochists* will even make sure that the rest of their family and friends are well aware that such a person couldn't do anything without them and will say that in front of the person concerned. That person will then feel doubly humiliated.

Masochists especially need to realize that they don't have to take up so much space in the life of their loved ones. On the other hand, they don't realize they take up so much space because it's often done so subtly. That's why their physical body takes up a lot of space. They get bigger in relation to the place they believe they should take up. Their body is there to reflect their belief. When *masochists* manage to feel deeply how special and important they are, they will no longer need to prove it to others. If they acknowledge themselves, their bodies will no longer need to take up so much space.

Masochists seem to be great controllers, but this need to control is essentially motivated by the fear of being ashamed of their loved ones or of themselves. This need for control is different from the control I speak of in the chapter on the wound of *betrayal*. A *masochist* mother will, for example, want to control the way her children and her partner dress, their appearance and cleanliness. This mother even wants her very young children to stay clean, and if she doesn't succeed, she'll feel ashamed as a mother.

As *masochists*, men and women often want to bond with their mothers - they'll do anything so their mothers won't be ashamed of them. Mothers have a great hold over *masochists,* although they are unaware of this and it isn't intentional. *Masochists* feel that their mothers are a real burden and this gives them another good reason to create a "solid back." This hold can continue even after the mother's death. *Masochists* often feel relieved or liberated when their mothers die, because they had let their mothers hamper their freedom. They do, however, feel ashamed of their relief. Only when the wound of *humiliation* is being healed does the mother's influence diminish.

Others want so much to bond that when their mothers die, instead of feeling liberated, they may have a severe attack of agoraphobia (for the description see p35). Unfortunately, these people are often treated for depression. As they're not treated for the right illness, it takes them a long time to get better. I explain in detail the difference between depression and agoraphobia in my book *Your Body Says: Love Yourself!*

Masochists find it hard to express their real needs or feelings because, since childhood, they have never dared speak for fear of being ashamed or of making someone else ashamed. *Masochists'* parents often told them that what went on in the home didn't concern strangers and so they weren't to speak about it. They had to keep everything to themselves. Shameful situations or family members had to be kept secret. You didn't, for example, speak about an uncle in prison, a cousin who was confined to a mental hospital or a family member who had committed suicide. For some people, even a homosexual brother is a shameful situation.

One man told me he was ashamed for having made his mother suffer so much when he was young because he once took some money out of her purse. In his opinion, it was inadmissible to do that to a mother who already went without for her children's sake. He had never told anyone. If you imagine hundreds of such hidden, "unmentionable" little secrets, you can understand why he suffered from throat and voice problems.

Some people have told me how ashamed they felt because they wished for things when they were young although they could see that their mothers went without the bare necessities. They never dared speak these wishes, especially to their mothers. *Masochists* generally get to the point where they are no longer in contact with their own desires because their desires might upset their mother.

They so want to please their mother that they are only in contact with the desires that will please *her*.

Masochists are generally over-sensitive and the least little thing hurts them. They therefore do everything possible not to hurt others. As soon as someone, especially someone they care for, feels unhappy, they feel responsible. They think they should have said or not said, done or not done something. They don't realize that by being so tuned in to the moods of others, they don't listen to their own needs. Of the five characters, *masochists* are those who least respect their own needs, even though they often know what they want. They make themselves suffer by not listening to their needs, which feeds their wound of *humiliation* and their *masochist* mask. They do everything to make themselves useful. It's a way for them to hide their wound and to make themselves believe they don't suffer from *humiliation*.

Masochists are frequently appreciated for their ability to make others laugh by laughing at themselves. They are very expressive when they talk and they find a way of making what they're saying sound funny. They also use themselves as targets for others to laugh at. It's an unconscious way of humiliating themselves, of putting themselves down. That way, no one will discover the fear of shame that is perhaps dissimulated under the words that make others laugh.

Masochists feel humiliated and put down at the slightest criticism. They see themselves as much smaller, less important than they really are. They can't imagine that others could consider them to be someone special and important.

One day I was with such a woman at a reception. She was well dressed and was wearing her most beautiful jewelry. I complimented her on the way she looked and she replied: *"I look like a fat, rich woman, don't you think?"*

When *masochists* use the word *fat,* it's to put themselves down, to humiliate themselves. When they dirty themselves while eating for example (which happens frequently), they say or think to themselves *"I'm such a pig!"*

A *masochist's* handwriting is often small; they take little steps, they like small cars, small houses, small objects, small mouthfuls, etc. I've noticed that they often use the word *little.* They say for example: *"Could you spare me a little of your time?"* or *"my little head"* or *"I've got a little idea"* or *"a little bit."* If you recognize yourself in the description of the *masochist* and you don't think you use these words, I suggest you ask the people around you to observe and listen to you. We are often the last to recognize ourselves.

People suffering from *humiliation* often blame themselves for everything, and even take the blame for others. It's their way of being good people. A *masochist* man told me that when his wife feels guilty about something, he is easily convinced that it's his fault. For example, his wife gave him a shopping list and forgot to write down an article that they buy every week. When he came back from the shops without the article, she said: *"Why didn't you remember to buy it? You know that we need that every week!"* He felt guilty and criticized himself for not having remembered the article. He didn't realize that she accused him because she felt guilty for having forgotten to put it on the list. Even if she had said: *"I forgot to put that article on the list"* he might still have blamed himself for having forgotten.

A woman with the same attitude was riding in a car with her husband. He was driving and they were talking. He looked at her to reply and at the same time, veered to the right. He accused his wife of distracting him and she felt guilty. When this type of situation occurs, she feels she has to say *"sorry."* While talking with her, I asked her if what he said was true, and if she did it on purpose. She realized that she was not at fault, but because he says she's guilty, she believes it.

These examples illustrate well how *masochists* take responsibility and blame themselves for things that don't belong to them. Taking the blame and saying *"sorry"* never solves anything because each time this situation arises, they blame themselves once again.

> ***It's important to remember that others can never make us feel guilty because guilt can only come from inside of us.***

Masochists often feel powerless with those they love and those close to them. When they are blamed (an attitude they attract in spite of themselves), they remain speechless, not knowing what to say to defend themselves. They blame themselves, and can suffer so much that they leave the situation. They will then try to justify and explain their behavior to bring back the peace. I'm not saying that only *masochists* feel guilty. Each of the five types feels guilty for different reasons. Because of the *humiliation* they go through, however, *masochists* seem to feel guilty more easily.

Freedom is very important to *masochists*. Being free means answering to no one, being controlled by no one, doing what we want when we want. When they were young, *masochists* hardly ever felt free, especially not with their parents. Their parents may have prevented them from having the friends they wanted, from going out when they wanted, or they may have been given a lot of responsibility at home, perhaps looking after the other children. I must say, however, that more often than not, they created their own obligations.

When *masochists* feel free and that no one is trying to hinder them, they have fun and live life to the fullest - they have no limits. During these times of freedom, they may go to the extreme in several areas of their lives. They may eat too much, buy too much food, cook too much, drink too much, do too much, want to help too much, work too much, spend too much, feel they have too much, talk too much. When they act like this, they feel ashamed because they feel humiliated by the looks or the comments of others. That's why they're very frightened of finding themselves with no limits; they are convinced they would do shameful things. Moreover, they believe that if they put themselves first, they wouldn't be useful to others. That revives the *humiliation* experienced when they were young and they dared to refuse to take care of others. That's why there is a lot of energy blocked in the body of a *masochist.* If they managed to allow themselves, without shame or guilt, to be as free as they need to be, their bodies would thin down from the release of energy.

A *masochist's* greatest fear is therefore freedom. They are convinced that they wouldn't be able to deal with being as free as they please. Therefore, they subconsciously organize themselves in such a way that they can't be free. Most of the time, they're the ones who choose the obligations or situations that tie them down. They think that if they make their own decisions, others can't control them; but their decisions often have the opposite effect, resulting in even more constraints and obligations. Here are a few examples:

- A man who feels free to have as many woman friends as he wants, at the same time creates a lot of problems for himself linked to managing to see all of them and make sure that none of them know about the others.

- A man feels trapped at home with his controlling wife. He therefore finds himself two or three extra evening jobs so he can get out. He believes he's free but in fact, he has no more free time to have fun or to see his child.

- A woman lives alone, and to be free, buys her own house. She has no more free time because she finds herself alone with all the work that has to be done. What *masochists* do to free themselves in one area imprisons them in another. On top of that, they create many situations in daily life where they are forced to do things that don't meet their needs.

Another characteristic of *masochists* is that they punish themselves believing they're punishing someone else. One woman told me that she frequently argued with her husband because he went out with his friends and wasn't with her often enough. She often ended these arguments by saying: *"If you're not happy you can go!"* He would then hurriedly take his coat and leave, and she was alone once more. By believing she was punishing him, she was in fact punishing herself and ended up alone again. As for her husband, he was only too happy to go out. What a good way to feed her *masochist* mask!

Masochists also have a gift for punishing themselves before someone else does. It's as if they want to give themselves the first lash of the whip, so that those to come will hurt less. This situation mainly arises when they're ashamed of something or when they fear they'll be ashamed in front of someone else. They find it so hard to please themselves that when they do take pleasure in being with someone or in doing something in particular, they criticize themselves for taking advantage. *Masochists* do everything they can to avoid being labeled as someone who takes advantage of other people. The more they accuse themselves of taking advantage, the bigger their bodies become.

A young mother once told me: *"I realize that I never manage to find time to enjoy myself or to enjoy what I'm doing."* She added that in the evening, when her husband and her children were watching television, she would sometimes stop to watch a little. When she was interested in the program she would watch it but remain standing. She didn't even manage to take time to sit down because, in her eyes, if she did, she would be lazy and so wouldn't be a good mother. A sense of duty is very important for *masochists*.

Masochists are often mediators between two people. They act as buffers between others, which is a reason for creating a good layer of protection. They also manage to be the scapegoat. A *masochist* mother will intervene, for example, if there's a problem between the father or the teacher and her children, instead of teaching her children to assume their responsibility. At work, *masochists* choose a job where they have to intervene to sort things out so that everybody is happy. Otherwise, they would criticize themselves for having done nothing and they would be ashamed because they feel responsible for other people's happiness or unhappiness. They even take on other peoples' responsibilities and commitments.

The fact that *masochists* take on too much, that they have too much weight on their shoulders, is reflected in their physique. Their shoulders become more and more hunched so that they can support everything - or they suffer from backache.

When *masochists* can no longer take on any more, the strain becomes visible in their body. Their skin looks as if it has been stretched to the limit, that there's no more room, that they're squashed in their bodies. When that's the case, they wear very tight-fitting clothes. It seems that if they breathe a bit too hard, their seams will rip. If this is happening to you, your body is trying to tell you that it's high time you healed your wound of *humiliation*, because you can't take anymore.

Masochists' appearance is important to them even though we could be led to think the opposite when we see the way some of them dress. In their heart of hearts, they like beautiful clothes and looking good, but as they believe they have to suffer, they don't allow themselves this luxury. When *masochists* dress so that their rolls of fat are visible in too-tight clothes, it's a sign that their wound is very deep. They make themselves suffer more. When they begin to allow themselves to go out and buy beautiful, good quality clothes that fit well, it's a sign that their wound is healing.

Masochists have the knack of attracting situations or people who will humiliate them. Here are a few examples:

- A woman who attracts a man who embarrasses her in public when he has drunk too much.

- A woman who attracts a partner who continually flirts with other women in front of her.

- A man who attracts a woman-friend who is vulgar, especially in front of his colleagues.

- A woman who stains her clothes either because she can't control her bladder or because her menstrual flow is too heavy.

- A person who dirties their clothes when eating in public; the man might stain his tie; the woman her bust. The woman will say that her big bosom gets in the way when she eats. She doesn't want to see that she attracts humiliating or shameful situations to help her discover her wound. How many times have I heard a *masochist* woman say to me during a meal: *"What a fat cow I am, I've stained myself again!"* The more they try to clean the stain, the bigger it seems to get!

⊚ A man is made redundant and while he's queuing for his unemployment benefit, he frequently sees a former colleague or someone he knows well who can see that he's queuing. He tries to hide.

Only people suffering from *humiliation* suffer the situations I've described and the examples I've given in this way. Another person, in the same situation may well have felt rejected, abandoned, betrayed or could have judged the situation as being unjust, but they wouldn't feel humiliated.

> ***That's why it's important to remember that it's not what we experience that makes us suffer but our reaction to what we experience, which is caused by our unhealed wounds.***

Masochists are often disgusted. They frequently create situations where they'll feel disgust toward themselves or others. They. In these situations, their first reaction is to reject those who disgust them. I've met several *masochists*, men and women, who were disgusted by their parents: a dirty mother, too fat, lazy or vulgar; an alcoholic father who chain smoked, smelled bad, or who went out with dubious friends or other women. Even when they were children, they didn't want to invite their friends over, which reduced their possibilities of having as many friends as others.

An illustration of how hard *masochists* find it to be in touch with their own needs is that you will frequently see them doing things for others that they wouldn't do for themselves. Here are a few examples:

- The man who helps his son paint his apartment even though he can't find the time to paint his own house.

- The woman who will clean her house from top to bottom when she's expecting guests but who won't clean her house when she's on her own, even though she prefers having a clean and tidy house. She doesn't feel important enough.

- The woman who likes being well dressed, will dress up when with others but when alone, she'll wear her "rags." If someone arrives unexpectedly, she'll feel ashamed at being seen like that.

As with the other wounds, human beings will do anything to remain oblivious to their suffering because they're too frightened of feeling the pain that goes with their wound. *Masochists* will do this by trying to be worthy at all costs. They often use the expression *to be worthy* and *to be unworthy*. They often consider themselves to be unworthy: for example, unworthy of being loved or of being acknowledged. As soon as they consider themselves to be unworthy, they feel they don't deserve to enjoy themselves; they deserve to suffer. Most of this goes on at an unconscious level.

Masochists generally have difficulties with their sexuality due to the guilt they feel. With all the taboos that make up children's sexual education, it's to be expected that people who are easily ashamed would be influenced by the notions of sin, trash, filth, etc. that are linked to sexuality.

Let's take the example of a child born of an unmarried mother. If the family circle considers this child to have been *born in sin*, the wound of *humiliation* will be awakened very early, so early in fact that he will suffer a very deep wound. From as early as conception, he will have a false image of the sexual act. I know that these days sexuality is freer and more open, but don't be misled. More and more teenagers are suffering from obesity, which prevents them from having a normal, pleasant, sex life. This sexual shame that is transmitted from generation to generation will only be eradicated when the wound of *humiliation* is healed. I've noticed over the years that most people suffering from *humiliation* are members of families where the whole family has a process to work through on the sexual level. All these souls didn't mutually attract one another for no reason.

Young *masochist* girls especially, tend to control themselves sexually, so that their mothers, who are generally very strict about this subject, won't be ashamed of them. The teenager learns that sex is disgusting and will have to do a lot of personal work to undo this belief. A young girl told me how ashamed she had been after a boy had kissed and touched her at the age of 14. The next day at school, she felt that everybody was looking at her and that they all knew what she had done.

How many young girls feel ashamed when their first menstrual cycle arrives and their breasts begin to grow!!! Some young girls even try to flatten their breasts when they find them too big.

Masochist teenage boys also feel controlled on the sexual plane. They're very frightened of getting caught when they masturbate. The more they find it shameful, the more they want to stop, the more inclined they'll be to masturbate. They'll also attract humiliating and shameful situations with their parents and friends on the sexual level. The *humiliation* is generally stronger with young girls and their mothers. The more someone feels that sex is shameful and dirty, the more they'll be likely to attract sexual harassment and abuse, especially during their childhood and teen years. They'll be so ashamed, they won't dare speak about it to anyone.

Several women of the *masochist* type have told me that once they had plucked up their courage to tell their mothers they were being subjected to harassment or incest, their mothers said things like: *"It's your fault, you're too sexy"* or *"You just shouldn't provoke people"* or *"You must surely have done something for that to happen to you."* This reaction from their mothers only amplifies their feeling of *humiliation*, shame and guilt. When a woman puts on protection in the form of an excess of weight around her hips, buttocks and stomach - in other words around the sexual area of her body - we can presume that she is frightened of sexuality, possibly because of previous abuse.

It's not surprising to see so many teenage girls and more and more teenage boys start to put on weight at the time their sexual desires awaken. It's a good way to be undesirable, avoid harassment, and subconsciously, deprive themselves of sexual pleasure. How many women have told me: *"If I had a beautiful, slim body, I would be too sexy and I might be unfaithful to my husband"* or *"I would dress more sexily and my husband would be jealous."* I've noticed that most fat people, men and women, are very sensual. Not only are *masochists* sensual, they are also sexual. However, as they don't feel that they deserve to enjoy themselves, they'll also manage to deprive themselves in the sexual area. They would make love often if they were able to let themselves be the way they would like to be, and especially if they took the time to discover their real needs in that field (as in all the other fields in fact). It is therefore probable that people suffering from *humiliation* have sexual fantasies but would never dare speak of them because they'd feel too ashamed. I've often heard women say that when they felt like making love, they didn't dare tell their partner. In their eyes it was unthinkable to disturb their partner for their own pleasure.

Generally speaking *masochist* men don't have the sort of sexual life they desire either. They are either very shy in regards to sex or obsessed, looking for it everywhere. They may find having an erection difficult or may suffer from premature ejaculation.

When *masochists* do allow themselves to enjoy sex and find a partner with whom they can let themselves go, it is still difficult for them to give themselves up totally. They're too ashamed to show what they like and are too ashamed to make sounds, for example, that would show how much they enjoy certain things.

Confession, required by certain religions, has also been a source of shame for some young people, especially for young girls who must confess intimate affairs to a man. They even have to confess "bad" thoughts. It's easy to imagine how difficult it must be, especially for a young *masochist* girl, to confess having made love before marriage. The most devout are very ashamed because GOD could see them, and disappointing GOD was inadmissible. They find it very humiliating to have to tell all that to a priest. This *humiliation* leaves a profound mark that can take many years to overcome.

Both male and female *masochists* have a hard time getting undressed in front of a new partner. They're worried that they'll be ashamed when their partner looks at them, even though deep down, *masochists* are those who most prefer to walk around naked when they manage to give themselves the right to do so. They may find sex "dirty," but because they are very sensual, they might also want to be more "dirty" themselves in their sexuality. This might be difficult for a *non-masochist* to understand. It's always easier to understand a wound when we experience it ourselves.

Here are a few examples of complaints and illnesses that *masochists* may suffer from:

- BACKACHE and the feeling of heaviness around the SHOULDERS is frequent because they take on so much. Their backache is especially due to the fact that they feel they lack freedom. The lower back is affected when it's linked to material things and the upper back is affected when it's linked to problems of affection.

- They can suffer from BREATHING PROBLEMS if they let themselves be suffocated by others.

- Problems in their LEGS and FEET, such as VARICOSE VEINS, SPRAINS and FRACTURES are frequent. Their fear of no longer being able to move makes them attract physical problems that really do prevent them from moving.

- They often suffer from LIVER problems because they worry themselves sick over others.

- Sore THROAT, TONSILLITIS, and LARYNGITIS are other problems that *masochists* have because they hold themselves back from saying what they have to say and above all, asking for what they want.

- The harder it is for them to be in touch with their needs and to make their requests, the more they increase the probability of having problems with their THYROID GLAND.

- Their inability to listen to their own needs often provokes ITCHY SKIN. We know that the expression: *"I'm itching to…"* means, *"I really want to…"* but *masochists* don't allow themselves to; it would be shameful to enjoy themselves too much.

- Another problem I've observed in *masochists* is a malfunction of the pancreas, which leads to HYPOGLYCEMIA and DIABETES. These illnesses appear in people who find it hard to treat themselves to sweet things or who feel guilty or are humiliated when they do.

- *Masochists* also have a predisposition to HEART PROBLEMS because they don't love themselves enough. They don't find themselves important enough to need enjoyment. The area of the heart has a direct link with our ability to enjoy ourselves "light-heartedly."

- Moreover, because they believe in suffering, *masochists* may have to undergo several OPERATIONS.

All the above-mentioned illnesses are explained in detail in my book *Your Body Says: Love Yourself!*

If you have one or several of these physical problems, it's very likely that they've been caused by the behavior of your *masochist* mask. These illnesses can also occur in people suffering from other wounds, but they seem to be much more common in people suffering from *humiliation*.

Masochists are often extremists when it comes to their diets. They prefer fatty foods, and often eat greedily, or they will eat small portions to try to make themselves believe they don't eat much (so they won't be ashamed of themselves). They will, however, eat several small portions, which in the end amounts to a lot. They have moments of bulimia, where they'll hide when they eat and will not really care what they are eating. They are able to eat standing up, for example. That way they believe that they've eaten less than they would have had they taken the time to sit down at the table.

Masochists generally feel very guilty and are ashamed to eat just about anything, especially if they consider it to be something that makes them put on weight - like chocolate, for example. A participant in a workshop told me that when she did her shopping at the grocery store and was at the cash desk, she would look at all the *treats* in her basket and would feel ashamed, imagining what all the people around her were thinking. She was convinced that they thought she was a *"fat pig."*

The fact that *masochists* think they eat too much doesn't help with their weight because, as you know, what we believe will happen, *happens*. The more we think we've eaten too much and the guiltier we feel, the more the food we've eaten will make us fat. If we eat a lot and don't put on weight, it's because our inner attitude and belief is different. Scientists will say that these two types of people have different metabolisms. It's true that we have different metabolisms and different glandular systems that can affect the physical body, but I'm convinced that our belief system determines our metabolism, glandular system and digestive system, and not the opposite.

Unfortunately, *masochists* reward themselves with food. It's their mainstay, their way of satisfying themselves. When they start to reward themselves differently, they won't feel such a strong need to compensate with food. They mustn't resent themselves for acting this way because it's surely saved them up to now, and helped them to be able to go on living.

According to statistics, 98% of those who go on a diet to lose weight put the lost weight back on plus a little extra, when they start eating normally again. Have you noticed that most people who want to get thinner say they want to *lose* weight or they have *lost* weight? It's part of human nature to do everything possible to regain what we have lost. That's why it would be preferable to use the expression *to be slimmer* rather than *to lose weight.*

I've noticed that after several diets, those who have lost weight and then put it back on have more and more difficulty losing weight, but it becomes easier and easier to put it on. It seems that the work we demand of them tires out our bodies. It's by far preferable to accept our weight and work on the wound of *humiliation* using the methods I've indicated in the last chapter of this book.

To become more conscious of their wound of *humiliation*, *masochists* must admit how ashamed they have been of themselves (or of others) and to what extent others may have been ashamed of them. They must, moreover, become conscious of how many times they humiliate themselves, put themselves down, and feel unworthy. As *masochists* are often extremists, they generally start off by seeing no situations where they felt shame - then later they may see enormous quantities. When that happens, their first reaction is to be shocked by all those situations of shame and *humiliation*, and then they laugh; the healing process has begun.

If you see yourself with the wound of *humiliation*, remember that the work you need to do to free yourself of this wound is with your soul. If you work only on the physical level, endlessly controlling yourself so that you don't put on or lose weight, you aren't following your life path and you'll have to be reincarnated in another body, perhaps an even bigger one. As long as you're here, it would be wiser to do what it takes to free your soul.

It's important to realize that your mother or father also suffered the wound of *humiliation*. They lived out this wound with their parent of the same sex as you. By feeling compassion for your parent, it'll be easier for you to feel compassion for yourself.

Remember that the main cause of a wound comes from our inability to forgive ourselves for what we do to ourselves or for what we do to others. It's difficult for us to forgive ourselves because most of the time we aren't even aware that we accuse ourselves. The deeper the wound, the more we humiliate ourselves by putting ourselves down or by comparing ourselves to others, or we humiliate others by being ashamed of them or by doing too much for them. We blame others for everything we do ourselves but don't want to see. That's why we attract people to us to show us what we are doing.

I mentioned earlier that the *masochist* mask appears to be the most difficult to recognize and to admit to. If you see yourself as having the physical characteristics of this mask, but not the others, I suggest you read this chapter several times in the coming months. Little by little, situations where you felt shame and *humiliation* will come to mind. It's important that you give yourself the necessary time to recognize this wound in you.

> ***Remember, the characteristics and the behavior mentioned in this chapter are only present when we wear our masochist mask, believing that in this way we'll avoid suffering from humiliation. Depending on the depth of the wound and the intensity of the pain, this mask can be worn for just a few minutes a week or almost all the time.***

The distinctive behavior of *masochists* is dictated by the fear of once again experiencing the wound of *humiliation*. It is, however, probable that you recognize yourself in some of the attitudes but not in everything I've written. It is almost impossible for one person to acknowledge all the attitudes and behavior patterns mentioned. Each wound has its respective inner behavior and attitudes. The thinking, feeling, speaking and acting that are linked to each wound, therefore show a reaction to what's happening in life. When we are reacting, we are not centered in our hearts and can't be happy. That's why it's so useful to be aware of those times we are being ourselves and when we're reacting. When we do this, we can become the masters of our lives instead of letting ourselves be controlled by our fears.

The aim of this chapter is to help you to become familiar with the wound of *humiliation*. If you see yourself in the description of the *masochist* mask, the last chapter contains all the information you'll need to heal this wound and to once again become yourself, without believing that the world is filled with *humiliation*. If you don't see yourself in this description, I suggest you check with those who know you well to see if they agree with you. I've already mentioned that it is possible to have just a small wound of *humiliation*. In this case, you might have only a few of the characteristics. Remember that it is important to go first by the physical description, because the physical body never lies, unlike us*+; we can easily lie to ourselves.

If you recognize people around you as suffering from this wound, you mustn't try to change them. Try to use what you learn in this book to develop more compassion for them, to understand their reactive behavior. It would be better that they read this book themselves, if they show an interest, rather than trying to explain the contents in your words.

Characteristics of the wound of
HUMILIATION

The awakening of the wound: Between one and three years old with the parent who took care of physical development, generally the mother. Lack of freedom. Feeling humiliated by that parent's control.

Mask: Masochist

Body: Fat, round, short waist, rounded chubby neck, tension in the neck, throat, jaw and pelvis. Round, open face. Many parts of the body are round and chubby.

Eyes: Big, round, open and innocent like those of a child.

Vocabulary: "worthy" "unworthy" "small" "fat"

Character: Frequently ashamed of themselves and of others or fear making someone ashamed of them. Don't like going fast. Know their needs but don't satisfy them. Take a lot on. Control to avoid shame. Believe they're unclean, heartless, pigs, beneath others. Need to bond. Make sure that they're not free because "being free" means "unlimited." If they have no limits, they're frightened of going too far. Play being mother. Oversensitive. Punish themselves believing they're punishing others. Want to be worthy. Feel disgust. Sensual, but ashamed on the sexual level and don't satisfy their needs. Compensate and reward themselves with food.

Greatest fear: Freedom

Eating habits: Like fatty foods, chocolate. Bulimic or several small portions. Ashamed of buying or eating "treats." Eat while standing up in order to believe that they haven't eaten a real meal (but they probably ate more than a normal meal).

Possible illnesses: Back problems, shoulders, throat, tonsillitis, laryngitis, breathing problems, legs, feet, varicose veins, sprains, fractures, liver, thyroid gland, itchy skin, hypoglycemia, diabetes, heart.

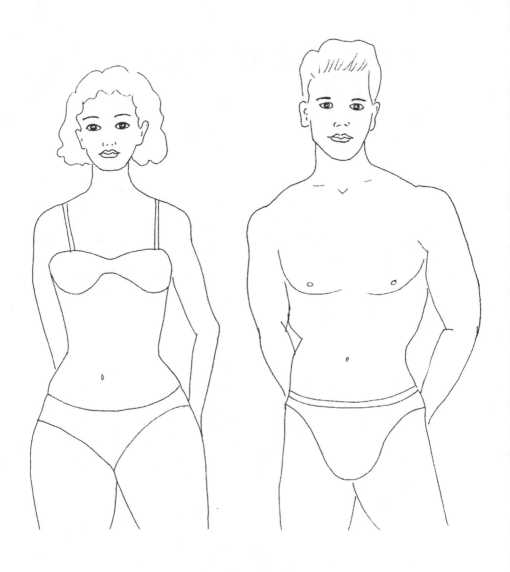

**Body of a person suffering
from the wound of BETRAYAL
(Controler mask)**

Chapter 5

Betrayal

We can betray someone or feel betrayed in many different ways. In the dictionary, to betray is *to stop being faithful to someone or to a cause, to abandon or to denounce.* The most important term linked to *betrayal* is *faithfulness,* which is the opposite of *betrayal.* To be faithful is to keep our promises, to be loyal and devoted. We can trust a faithful person. When that trust is broken, we may feel betrayed.

This wound is awakened between the ages of two and four when our sexual energy is developing. This wound is experienced with the parent of the opposite sex. The soul who wants to heal this wound attracts a parent with whom there will be a strong love bond, great mutual attraction and, therefore, a strong *Oedipus complex.*

Here is a short explanation of the Oedipus complex for those who want to know more about the theory that was elaborated by the psychoanalyst SIGMUND FREUD. According to Freud, we all have this complex but at different levels. All children fall in love with their parent of the opposite sex, or with the person who plays that role, between the ages of two and six - because this is the age at which sexual energy develops. From then on, they come into contact with their life force, their sexual force, the force that represents their creative capacity.

It's natural that from birth, babies bond with their mothers and need their attention and care. Their mothers, however, have to continue their everyday occupations and look after the other members of the family, just as they did before their babies were born. If the mother pays *too much* attention to the baby's whims, to the point of almost becoming their slave, the child begins to believe that they can replace their father and that they alone can satisfy their mother. In this case, according to Dr. Freud, the child won't go through the Oedipal phase that's essential to their development. This will be very unhealthy for the child on the psychological and sexual levels when they become an adult.

As children, we can go through an Oedipal phase rather well when we realize that if we hadn't had a father, we wouldn't exist. Even if he isn't present, mothers must make their children understand that they have a father and that he is as important as they are. As soon as children realize that they were conceived through a union of the two sexes, they develop an interest for the opposite sex. They develop a subconscious desire to make a baby with their parent of the opposite sex. At the same time, they develop their creative power. This explains why little girls try to seduce their fathers and little boys, their mothers. They do everything possible to win the affection of the parent of the opposite sex. They will also try to protect that parent, even if they're disappointed because they don't receive the desired attention. When the parent of the same sex as the child hurts the parent of the opposite sex, the child suffers. Some even go so far as to wish the offending parent would die.

Unfortunately, most of the time, the Oedipus complex is not integrated because the mother is too possessive of her son and the father of his daughter. The more the father is put down (by the mother) or ignored, as is sometimes the case, the more difficult it will be to resolve this complex. I've observed that those who suffer from *betrayal* didn't solve their Oedipus complex when they were young. This means that their dependence on the parent of the opposite sex is far too strong; this will affect their affective and sexual relationships later in life. They will tend to compare their partner with their parent of the opposite sex or will expect too much from their partner, hoping to receive what they didn't receive from that parent. When making love, they'll find it difficult to give themselves up entirely. They'll hold back because they're afraid of being deceived.

The soul that incarnates to heal the wound of *betrayal* chooses parents who are fairly self-centered and who charm their children. With this type of parent, children are led to believe that their parents need them, and they want to make their parents feel good, especially their parent of the opposite sex. They do everything to become special to that parent. A man suffering from the wound of *betrayal* told me that when he was young, his mother and his two sisters made him feel important by telling him only he could make shoes shine so well when he cleaned them, and only he could make the floor shine so well when he washed and waxed it. He, therefore, felt special when he did these two chores. He didn't realize they were using charm to manipulate him. This is an example of the way we can unconsciously feel betrayed when young.

Children feel betrayed by their parent of the opposite sex each time that parent makes a promise that isn't kept, and each time that parent betrays their trust. They especially feel betrayed if their love or their sexuality is abused. For example, in nearly all cases an incestuous act is experienced as *betrayal*. Children also experience *betrayal* each time they sense that their parent of the same sex feels betrayed by the other parent. They feel this *betrayal* as strongly as if it had happened to them. A little girl can also experience *betrayal* if she feels that her father pays less attention to her when another baby is born.

When children begin to experience *betrayal*, they create the CONTROLLER mask to protect themselves. The type of control that *controllers* use has a different motivation than the control *masochists* exert. *Masochists* control to avoid feeling ashamed, or so that other people won't be ashamed of them. *Controllers*, on the other hand, control to make sure they keep their promises, are faithful and responsible, or to make sure other people keep their commitments.

Controllers create a body for themselves that radiates strength and power and seems to say: "*I'm responsible, you can trust me.*" We can recognize a male *controller* by his broad shoulders, broader than his hips. (Sometimes there isn't a great difference between the width of the shoulders and the width of the hips but, as I said in another chapter, you must follow your intuition.) When, at first glance, you feel that more strength exudes from the top half of a man's body than the lower half, it's a sign that he suffers from *betrayal*. On the other hand, if you see a man with nice broad shoulders, large biceps, a muscular chest, who's wearing a tight T-shirt to show off his muscles, you can be sure that he has a very strong wound of *betrayal*. Female *controllers'* strength is concentrated around the hips, buttocks, stomach and thighs. Women who suffer from this wound are often pear-shaped; the bottom half of their bodies is generally wider than their shoulders. The more accentuated the large part of the pear, the deeper the wound of *betrayal*.

In some cases, however, the opposite phenomenon can be observed. A man may have hips and thighs that are wider than his shoulders, and a woman may have a man's body; that is to say, wide shoulders and slim hips and thighs. After much observation and checking with several of these cases, I concluded that these *controllers'* wounds of *betrayal* were experienced with their parent of the *same* sex rather than with their parent of the opposite sex. Their Oedipus complex, therefore, hadn't been lived out conventionally; i.e. with the parent of the opposite sex. The people concerned became very attached to the parent of the same sex, almost to the point of ignoring the other parent. These cases, however, are rather rare. That's why this chapter refers to the wound of *betrayal* being linked to the parent of the opposite sex. If you consider yourself to be in the opposite case, all you need to do is to invert the sex of the parent who awakened the wound.

However, if a woman is feminine and her shoulders are wider than her hips, this indicates the wound of *rejection* because a 'piece' of her hips is missing.

On the whole, people wearing the *controller* mask have their place in life. They are very physical, and often have a *look at me* aura. They are often overweight but they don't look fat. They would more generally be qualified as *strong people*. This person doesn't look fat from behind, but seen from the front they may have a big stomach. It's their way of showing their strength with a stomach that says: *"I'm capable."* Eastern countries call this the *hara power*.

I would like to specify that putting on weight is always linked to the mental plane. It happens to those who believe that they don't fully have their place in life. Being overweight, therefore, doesn't uniquely apply to the wound of *humiliation*, which I described in the previous chapter. For *masochists,* excess weight is another way to feel humiliated. For the other wounds, putting on weight is rather linked to the belief that they should take up more space. We can see that *withdrawers* and *dependents* - who are very slim, thin even - don't want to take up more space. Through their *lack* of weight, the *withdrawer* can be more invisible and the *dependent* can appear to be weaker, and therefore in need of help.

Remember that when we have only a few of the characteristics mentioned it's because our wound is not so deep. We can see in which area a person controls and fears being betrayed by the part of their body that indicates strength or power. For example, men or women with large hips and a large stomach, often feel rage towards the opposite sex, especially on the sexual level. These people may well have been sexually harassed when younger or were victims of sexual abuse, so they created sexual protection in the form of excess weight around those parts of their bodies.

If you see indications of the *controller* in your physical body, but consider yourself to be rather introverted, it's likely you will have difficulty seeing in yourself the following characteristics. This is because the control you exert is a lot more subtle and hidden, therefore more difficult to recognize. If this is the case, the people who know you well will be able to tell you, after reading the following paragraphs, if you wear the *controller* mask. When people are more extroverted, their control is more apparent and easier to see.

Strength is a characteristic that is common to all people suffering from the wound of *betrayal*. They find it hard to accept any form of *betrayal*, whether it is on their part or on the part of others, so do everything possible to be responsible, strong, special and important. *Controllers* thus satisfy the ego that doesn't want to see how many times a week they betray themselves or others. Most of the time, they're unaware of what they are doing. *Betrayal* is so unacceptable to them that they can't believe they could be capable of such a thing. If they are aware that they have betrayed someone, by breaking a promise, for example, they find all sorts of excuses and may even lie to get out of it. For example, if they forget to do something, they'll swear that they had thought about it and they will have (or will invent) an excuse for not having done it.

Remember that each of our wounds exists to remind us that if others make us suffer, it's because we do the same thing to ourselves or to others. The ego can neither understand nor accept this. If you see yourself as having the *controller* mask and you feel resistance when reading these lines, it's your ego that's resisting, not your heart.

Of the five masks, *controllers* are those who expect the most of others because they like to be able to plan everything, thus be in control. I mentioned in another chapter that *dependents* also expect a lot from others but their expectations are linked to their need to be helped and supported, which is in turn linked to their wound of *abandonment*. *Controllers'* expect others to do what they're supposed to be doing, to be trustworthy. They are, moreover, very clever at guessing other people's needs. They often say what they know others would like to hear, but without really intending to do what they have just said.

Controllers have strong personalities. They say what they believe with conviction and expect others to adhere to their beliefs. They quickly form their opinions, of people or situations, and are convinced that they are right. They express their opinions categorically and want to convince others at all costs. They will often use the expression *"Do you understand?"* to make sure that they were well understood. They believe that when other people understand them, it means they agree; this unfortunately is not always the case. I checked with several *controllers* to see if they realized how hard they tried to convince me when they expressed their opinions; they said no. All the masks have one point in common: we don't realize when we are wearing one. Those around us, on the other hand, see the mask that we are wearing a lot more easily.

Controllers make sure that they're never in conflicting situations where they won't be able to control. When they're with people they consider fast and strong, they stay in the background for fear they might not be able to match them.

Controllers act quickly. They understand, or want to understand rapidly and they find it hard when others take their time to explain or to say something. They often interrupt and answer before the other person has finished. If, on the other hand, someone dared do the same to them, they would say vehemently: *"Let me finish, I haven't finished what I wanted to say."*

Controllers are very talented and act fast. They therefore have little patience with people who are slower. For example, following a slow driver often gets on their nerves and makes them angry. They have to make a real effort to let it go. This is often a time when they try to control others. *Controller* parents will demand that their children be quick and learn quickly. They demand the same of themselves. When things don't go fast enough, and especially when they are bothered by something they hadn't planned for, they get angry. They like finishing first, especially if they're in competition. Finishing first is even more important than doing well. They may even go so far as to change the rules of a game to their advantage.

When things don't go as they would like, *controllers* can easily become aggressive, even though they don't see themselves as such. They see themselves as assertive, strong, and refusing to be walked over. Of the five characters, *controllers* are those who will have the most ups and downs. One minute they can be full of love, and the next, they can be angry for no apparent reason. Their close ones don't know where they stand; they often feel betrayed by this volatile attitude.

Controllers have to work on their patience and toler- ance, especially when they are prevented from working or doing things their way. For example, they'll do everything to get better if they are ill, so that they can get on with what they were doing. When their close ones or those who have commitments to them are ill, they become impatient.

Controllers often "futurize"; in other words, they try to plan everything for the future. Their mental plane is very active. The stronger the wound, the more they want to anticipate the future and control everything to avoid suffering from *betrayal*. Because they want everything to happen as they have planned, and so are full of expecta- tions for the future, they are unable to live in the present. For example, while they're working, they'll be busy plan- ning their future holidays and when they're on holiday, they'll plan their return to work or worry about what's go- ing on at home during their absence.

Controllers like arriving early so that they can con- trol everything. They don't like being late and don't toler- ate others arriving late even though trying to change others gives them an opportunity to control. They get an- noyed if they finish a job late or if someone else is late with a promised task. As they are demanding, they often don't give themselves, or others, enough time to do the job. This problem is especially experienced with people of the opposite sex, with whom they are more easily annoyed.

Controllers find it hard to trust others and to delegate. They continually check what the other is doing to make sure it's done according to their expectations. They also have problems when they have to show someone who learns slowly how to do something. When they delegate something, they delegate easy jobs or jobs where they won't be blamed if they're not done properly. That's why *controllers* have to be fast: they do nearly everything themselves and also spend time checking up on those who help them. They seem to have eyes and ears everywhere so they can make sure that others are doing what they're supposed to be doing. *Controllers* are more demanding of others than of themselves. However, they find it easier to trust someone of the same sex so they control more closely those of the opposite sex. I would like to remind you that the wound of *betrayal* that *controllers* suffer from is awakened each time they encounter people who don't respect their commitments.

Controllers consider themselves to be hard workers and responsible and so have problems with laziness. According to them, you can only laze around once you have finished doing everything you are responsible for, not before. Seeing others, especially of the opposite sex, doing nothing really gets on their nerves. They call them lazy and find it hard to trust them. They also make sure that everyone knows everything *they* have done, how much they did and how they did it; that way others will see how responsible and trustworthy they are. *Controllers* hate not being trusted. They consider themselves as being so responsible and talented that others should naturally trust them. What they don't see, however, is how hard it is for them to trust others.

It's important for people wearing the *controller* mask to show their strength and above all, their courage. They are very demanding of themselves because they want to show others what they're capable of. Any act of cowardice, any act that shows a lack of courage is a form of *betrayal* in their eyes. They would be very angry with themselves if they dropped a project, if they didn't have the courage to see it through to the end. They can't accept cowardice in themselves or in others.

Controllers find it hard to confide in anyone because they fear that one day what they reveal will be used against them. They really have to trust someone before they confide in that person. They, however, are the first to repeat to others what has been confided to them but, it goes without saying, they have a very good reason for doing so.

They like to add their comments to what others are saying or doing. For example, if a mother is scolding her child, the *controller* father, while walking past, will add: *"Have you understood what your mother just said?"* The situation doesn't even concern him but he interferes anyway. If it's his daughter being reprimanded, and he agrees with her mother, it's highly likely that she'll feel betrayed, especially if she's Daddy's little girl and Daddy doesn't defend her when Mummy punishes her. *Controllers* generally like to have the last word; that's why they always find something to add to everything...or nearly everything.

Controllers like to get involved in other people's business. As they quickly see everything that's going on around them and they feel they're stronger than others, they like to take care of everything. They believe they have to help others organize their lives. They don't realize that they do this from a need to be in control. By taking care of others, they can control what the others will do to them, how and when they'll do it. When *controllers* take care of other people's problems, it's because they feel that the others are weaker. It's a veiled way of showing their strength. As long as we don't really believe in our own strength, we'll do everything to try to prove it to others, such as taking care of those who are "weaker."

Moreover, *controllers* are very sensitive but their sensitivity doesn't show through because they are too busy showing their strength. We saw in the previous chapters that *dependents* take care of others to gain their support and that *masochists* take care of others to be good people and so that nobody will be ashamed of them. *Controllers* take care of other people's business so that they won't suffer from *betrayal*, or to make sure that the others will satisfy their expectations. If you see yourself as the type of person who feels responsible for sorting out the life of all those you love, I suggest you examine your motivation closely.

Controllers' egos easily get the upper hand when someone corrects what they're doing because they don't like being watched, especially not by another *controller*.

They have big problems with authoritarian people because they believe that these people want to control them. They justify themselves and always have a good reason for doing things their way. They find it hard to admit their fears and don't want to speak about their weaknesses. Moreover, *controllers* start saying: "I'm capable, let me do it by myself," at a very young age. They want to do things their way and are happy when others acknowledge them, congratulate them and above all notice what they're doing.

They don't want to show their vulnerability for fear someone might take advantage of them and control them. They like to appear brave, courageous and strong as often as possible.

Generally *controllers* do exactly as they please. They tell others what they want to hear but don't respect what they say. Here's an example. One day, my husband and I hired a *controller* type person to do some work at the house. I explained what I wanted done and how I wanted him to start but could see that he didn't agree and didn't like my telling him what to do, because he was the expert in repairs. He therefore tried to convince me that the way he saw things was best, without taking our priorities into consideration. I told him that I understood his point of view but, for our needs, my husband and I preferred something different. He replied: *"Very well."* Two days later, however, I discovered that he had done as he pleased. When I told him how annoyed I was that he hadn't done as I asked, he had lots of reasons to justify his decision. He managed to have the last word because it was too late to start over again.

I mentioned earlier that *controllers* don't like authoritarian people but don't realize how often they give orders or decide for others. I enjoy observing *controllers* who are managers or supervisors in public places such as restaurants, hospitals, shops etc. They want to know everything that's going on; they give their opinions without being asked; they seem unable to stop themselves from commenting on what others are saying or doing.

One day I was observing a *controller* type waiter in a restaurant. He was attacking another waiter who had all the characteristics of a *withdrawer*. The *controller* was continually telling the *withdrawer* who he should serve and what he should do. The *withdrawer* raised his eyebrows in exasperation. I had just told my husband what was happening, saying that the two of them might end up by having a row, when the young *withdrawer*, who was serving us, came to our table and started telling us how difficult the situation was for him and that he intended to leave his job fairly soon.

Knowing the different wounds well, I wasn't surprised by his words because a *withdrawer* who feels too rejected prefers to withdraw rather than face the situation. The most interesting part of this story is that the *controller* wasn't even the boss or his supervisor. He was a waiter just like the *withdrawer*. He had just decided to make the other waiter as good as he was. The *controller* seemed to have the situation in hand and controlled the customers well. He seemed to be very proud of himself and didn't seem to realize how he controlled. In his opinion, the other waiter should have appreciated his help. What we call control, *controllers* call help.

As my husband and I frequently eat in restaurants when we're traveling, I find it very useful to recognize the different wounds as it helps me to know how to approach waiters. For example, I know that if I make an unpleasant remark to a *controller* type waiter or if I tell him that he's made a mistake, he'll start justifying himself immediately and may even lie to save his reputation and not lose face. If I have a controlling approach with him, I won't obtain what I want. He has to feel it comes from him and not that it is imposed on him. I've even been in the situation where waiters made me wait on purpose, just to show me that they would have the last word.

When someone tries to convince *controllers* of a new idea, they are generally skeptical. The most difficult thing for them is to be taken by surprise and not to have had enough time to prepare. Being unprepared, they run the risk of not being in control and consequently of being controlled.

As surprise is a difficult emotion for *controllers* to handle, their first reaction is to withdraw and remain alert. They prepare for every possibility and like to imagine every option so that they'll be ready. They don't realize how often they can change *their* minds and put their loved ones in situations where there is a last minute decision that will take them by surprise. They give themselves the right to change their minds easily and often.

A woman suffering from the wound of *betrayal* told me that when she was young, she always tried to guess her father's reactions - reactions that made her suffer. When she expected her father to hit her because she'd been naughty, he didn't. When she expected praise for her good marks at school, he would hit her and she couldn't work out why he was angry. This example illustrates well how she attracted this type of behavior because of her wound, and that her father adopted his behavior because of *his* wound of *betrayal*. It's as if he derived great pleasure from taking her by surprise and not satisfying her needs (that he seemed to know in advance). This can be explained by the bond that exists between a father and his daughter or between a mother and her son who suffer from this type of wound. Any unpredictable behavior on the part of the parent usually generates a feeling of *betrayal* on the part of the *controller* type child.

Controllers are quick to call others hypocrites because they are so distrustful. On the other hand, they could often be thought of as hypocrites for the way they manipulate others. For example, when things aren't going their way, they will get angry and speak behind the concerned person's back to anyone who will listen. They don't realize that at times like these, they too are hypocrites.

Controllers hate being lied to. They'll say: *"I'd rather be hit than lied to."* They frequently lie themselves, but in their eyes, they're not really lying. They can easily find good reasons for bending the truth. They think their lies, which are generally subtle, are necessary for them to get their way or to justify themselves. For example, I mentioned earlier that they can easily guess other people's expectations and frequently say what others want to hear. Unfortunately, they can't always keep their word because they commit themselves without checking to see if they'll be able to keep their commitments. They therefore find all sorts of good excuses; they may even say that they don't remember having committed themselves. The others know they have been lied to and feel betrayed. *Controllers* don't see this as a lie at all. They may qualify this type of behavior as an expression of their limits, for example. Paradoxically, they find it very difficult when someone doesn't believe them. If someone doesn't trust them, they feel betrayed. They do everything possible to make people trust them to avoid this painful feeling of *betrayal*.

In my workshops, several women have complained that their husbands manipulated and controlled them through lies. After listening to the description of their husbands, I realized that most of these men were *controllers*. I'm not saying that all *controllers* lie but it's more probable that a *controller* will lie than anyone else. If you see yourself as suffering from this wound, I strongly suggest you be attentive because more often than not, liars don't believe that their lies are real lies, or else they don't even realize they're lying. You could even ask those who know you well if they think you sometimes lie or if they hear you lying.

Controllers can't tolerate cheating in others. On the other hand, if they cheat at cards, for example, they'll say that it was for fun or to see if the others would notice. If they cheat on their tax return, they say that everyone does it.

Moreover, *controllers* don't like being placed in a situation where they must report on someone else - a work colleague, for example. They know that when someone else does the same to them, they feel betrayed. They there-

fore don't want to do it to others. A few years ago at the
LISTEN TO YOUR BODY offices, there was a new employee who was supposed to provide information to cli-
ents over the phone and often gave them inexact
information. This had been going on for a few weeks before another employee informed me about it. I checked
with the employee who worked next to her to see if he'd
noticed what was going on, and he said that he'd known
from the beginning, but that *telling on people* wasn't part
of his job. Suffering from the wound of betrayal myself,
this experience made me angry because I feared for my
company's reputation.

In fact, *controllers'* reputations are very important to
them. If someone says or does anything that could affect
their good reputation, they feel insulted and angry because they feel they have been horribly betrayed. They'll
go as far as lying to keep their good reputation. What they
value above all is their reputation for being reliable, responsible people who take good care of their affairs.
When they speak of themselves, they don't reveal themselves entirely. They only speak of things that will en-
hance their reputation.

They even find it hard to guarantee a loan for someone because they fear for their reputation if that person
doesn't pay. If, after thinking it through, they decide to do
it, and that person doesn't respect the payments, *controllers* feel horribly betrayed. *Controllers* don't like going
into debt, and when they're in debt, they pay as quickly as
possible to keep their good reputation.

I've also noticed that *controller* parents frequently act to protect their reputation, rather than the best interests of their children. They'll try to convince their children that whatever they've done is for the children's good, but children aren't fools. They know when their parents are really thinking about themselves. *Controller* parents want to decide for their children, whereas parents who really think about their children's happiness take the time to speak to them about what would really make them happy.

Controllers don't like to find themselves in situations where they can't answer a question. That's why, on the whole, they like learning about many different subjects. When they're asked a question they try to answer, even if it means making something up, because it's very difficult, if not impossible, for them to say: *"I don't know."* The other person may realize immediately that they didn't know the answer, and think that they lied. When someone says: *"I didn't know…"* controllers will nearly always feel the need to reply: *"I did. I don't know where I learned that, but I knew."* or *"I learned that at such and such a place."* Unfortunately, it's not always true. *I knew that* is an expression often used by *controllers*.

Controllers feel insulted if someone interferes in their affairs without permission. They can get very angry, for example, if someone reads their mail. If someone intervenes or speaks on their behalf while they are present, they will feel insulted because they believe the other person doesn't trust their ability. They don't realize that they often intervene and speak for others. For example, a *controller* married to a *dependent* woman (the wound of *abandonment*) may always be telling her how and why she should do this or that. Unfortunately, this type of woman suffers in silence.

I must add that in a couple where one of the partners is a *controller* and the other is a *dependent,* the *controller* is very often dependent on the partner's weakness or dependency. *Controllers* believe they're strong because they control others, but in fact it's another form of dependency. When two *controllers* live together, it's a relationship based on power struggles.

For *controllers,* all the examples I've mentioned are seen as forms of *betrayal.* If you're surprised, it's because your definition of the word "betrayal" may be too limited. It took me years of hard work before I realized this. I could see that my own body showed the wound of *betrayal,* but I couldn't find the links between what was going on in my life and this wound. I found it especially hard to find the link with my father, with whom I had a strong Oedipus complex. I adored him so much that I couldn't see how I could possibly have felt betrayed by him and I certainly couldn't admit that I had resented him.

After several years, I was finally able to admit that my father didn't live up to my definition of a *responsible man.* I come from a family where the women generally make the decisions and the men help them. That's how it was with my parents and with my uncles and aunts. I therefore concluded that the women had all the responsibilities because they were stronger and more capable. In my eyes, the men were weak because they didn't control anything. In fact, my concept was false; just because someone doesn't make decisions doesn't mean they are not responsible. I also had to redefine the words *responsibility* and *commitment*.

When I took the time to think over what had happened during my childhood, I realized that my mother did make most of the decisions, but my father always remained committed to her and assumed his responsibilities. When one of my mother's decisions didn't turn out to be the best, my father assumed the consequences as much as she. He *was* therefore a responsible man.

To help me understand the notion of responsibility, I attracted a first husband and two sons whom I considered irresponsible and tried for a long time to control. I then realized that this was my general opinion of all men, which explained why I was wary with members of the opposite sex. To help me cure my wound of *betrayal*, I attracted a second husband who also suffered from *betrayal*. Thanks to him, I can see the progress I'm making daily, and consequently, the healing of my wound. I can see a great difference in the way I act with him and the way I acted with my ex-husband.

Controllers are also afraid of commitment, and this fear comes from a greater fear: the fear of that commitment being broken. They believe that not keeping your word and breaking a commitment are synonymous with *betrayal*. They therefore feel they have to keep their word and if they over commit themselves, they feel trapped. So rather than breaking their commitments, they prefer not to make any. I know someone who always demands that others promise to phone him. On top of that, he wants to know what day and at what time they're going to call. If they forget to phone him, he then calls them to tell them what he thinks of them. He doesn't realize that he demands a lot of others, but at the same time, he doesn't commit himself at all, or at least, not sufficiently. When I observe him, I see how much energy he uses trying to control everything. This behavior only feeds his wound of *betrayal*.

> **Many of those who suffer from the wound of betrayal have felt that their parent of the opposite sex didn't keep their commitments and live up to the child's expectations of an ideal parent.**

An example that comes to mind is that of a 60-year-old man who lived alone with his mother when he was a child. She went out with any man who would willingly spend money on her. When he was fifteen, his mother went off with one of these men who was prepared to spend a fortune on her. She put her son into boarding school, which caused him to feel abandoned and above all, betrayed. When he grew up, he attracted women by spending money on them and never really committed himself to any of them. He thought by doing this he was taking revenge on his mother, but in fact, he has the same wound to heal as the men he judged badly for seducing his mother with their money.

It is also fairly common to hear participants in my workshops say that when they discovered they were pregnant and the prospective father was afraid of commitment, he strongly insisted that they abort. When this happens to women suffering from the wound of *betrayal*, it adds another layer to their wound. It's very difficult for them to accept that their partner refuses to take responsibility for his unborn child.

I mentioned earlier that *controllers* don't trust easily. They are, however, more trusting if there is no sexual involvement. They are very seductive, but as long as they have a deep wound, they prefer to be friends, rather than lovers, with members of the opposite sex. They feel more confident with friends. They often use their charm to manipulate others and, generally speaking, they manage quite well. When I speak of charm, I don't necessarily mean charm on a sexual level; they can use charm in all areas of their lives. The *controller* will, for example, be his mother-in-law's favorite son-in-law because he will have charmed her with his sweet-talk. On the other hand, *controllers* are very wary in the presence of another charmer. They know immediately when someone is trying to charm them and they don't buy it. *Controllers'* greatest fear is dissociation in all its forms. They're the ones who find it the hardest to accept a separation, as this is a form of dissociation. For *controllers,* it's a serious defeat. If they are the ones who want the separation, they'll worry about betraying their partner and about being called a traitor. If the partner wants the separation, they'll accuse them of *betrayal.* Moreover, a separation will remind them that they weren't in control of the relationship. It does seem, however, that *controllers* go through separations and breakups more often than others. They also fear commitment because they fear separation. This fear often leads them to attract love affairs where their partners aren't free to commit. It's a good way for them to hide from the fact that *they* don't want to commit themselves.

When two *controllers* live together and things aren't going well, they constantly put off the moment of truth, where they admit that it would be better to separate. When they form a couple, they are all one, or all the other. Either they bond completely and feel that they're part of the other person, or they feel dissociated, especially when they feel their partners don't appreciate them. For *controllers*, being dissociated means feeling torn or separate from the other. In fact, they often use the word *dissociated* when they speak. They'll say, for example, "*I feel dissociated from my body.*" A woman once told me that when she and her husband had a misunderstanding, she felt as if she'd been cut in half - she was desperate, fearing a separation.

From my observations, the majority of *controllers* develop the wound of *abandonment* before developing the wound of *betrayal*. Those who decide, when young, not to accept their *dependent* side (their wound of *abandonment*) develop the necessary strength to hide their wound of *abandonment*; that's when they start developing the *controller* mask. If we look closely at these people, we can see the *dependent* mask in their eyes (sad or drooping eyes), or their mouth droops, or one or more parts of their body sags or lacks muscle tone.

It's easy to imagine small children who, when feeling abandoned or lacking in attention, decide to use everything in their power to charm their parent of the opposite sex, to try to attract their attention and especially to feel supported by that parent. These children convince themselves that they're so kind and adorable that their parent will have no choice but to take special care of them. The more they try to control their parent that way, the more expectations they have. When nothing happens, when their expectations are dashed, they feel betrayed. They therefore try to control more and more. They build a strong shell for themselves, believing that thus protected, they won't suffer from any future *betrayal* or *abandonment*. Their *controller* part encourages their *dependent* part to want to become independent.

For some people it's the wound of *abandonment* that is stronger than the wound of *betrayal*, for others, it's the opposite and the *controller* mask predominates. In the chapter on *abandonment* we mentioned a man who develops beautiful muscles through weight lifting, but whose body becomes flabby when he stops doing his exercises. He is a good example of a person who has both a wound of *betrayal* and a wound of *abandonment*.

You may see yourself as having the *controller* mask, but not the *dependent* mask. I advise you, however, not to eliminate this possibility. Remain open to the idea that you might also have a wound of *abandonment*. The wound that is dominant in the body is the wound that is being activated most often in our everyday lives.

Based on the observations I've made over the years, it has become clear that we can suffer from *abandonment* without necessarily suffering from *betrayal*, but if we suffer from *betrayal*, we also suffer from *abandonment*. I've also observed that many of those whose bodies show the wound of *abandonment* when young begin to develop the characteristics of the wound of *betrayal* when they get older. The opposite can also occur. The body is always changing; it shows us at all times what is happening inside.

You may have noticed that those who are afraid of being abandoned and those who are afraid of being betrayed have several points in common. In addition to those already mentioned, they both like to attract attention. *Dependents* do it to get attention and to be taken care of, whereas *controllers* do it to control a situation, to show their strength of character and to impress others. Actors and singers are very often of the *dependent* type, and comedians, humorists and those who like making others laugh are generally of the *controller* type. The two character types like being the star but for different reasons. *Controllers* often have the reputation of taking up a lot of space. They don't generally like their partner to be in the forefront.

One woman told me that as long as she and her husband were business associates, everything was fine between them. As soon as she decided to set up on her own and was more successful than her husband, even though it wasn't in the same field, the relationship deteriorated. It became a competition. The husband felt betrayed and she blamed herself for having abandoned him.

Another characteristic that defines *controllers* is their great difficulty in making a choice when they feel that they might lose something through that choice. This explains why *controllers* sometimes find it difficult to make up their minds or are accused of thinking too much. When they are sure of themselves, especially sure of being able to control the situation, they have no problems making a decision.

A *controller's* difficulty with separation also shows at work. If they run their own company, they can go as far as putting themselves into tricky situations - heavy debt, for example - before admitting that they can no longer continue. As employees, *controllers* often have management positions. It's always difficult for them to leave a company. The opposite is also true. When a trustworthy employee decides to leave, a *controller* finds it very hard to let them go, and often feels angry and aggressive.

Controllers are generally born leaders, and like being in charge of others. They don't want to stop controlling because they believe that if they do, they will no longer be in charge. In fact, the opposite is true. When *controllers* stop controlling and content themselves with managing, they become much better bosses. There is a big difference between controlling and managing. When we control, we do so using the influence of fear. To manage is to give direction, without necessarily wanting things to be done our way. We can be managers and still learn things from our subordinates.

Controllers' natural leadership often leads them to become company directors, but their expectations and the control they exert cause them a lot of stress. It's as hard for *controllers* to let go as it is urgent and necessary that they do so.

Another of the great fears that haunts *controllers* is to be cast aside which, to them, is *betrayal*. They don't realize, however, how often they cast others aside by eliminating them from their lives. For example, they won't give someone another chance if they no longer trust them. Quite often, they won't even want to speak to that person again. When they're angry, and especially when things don't go as they expect, they can easily hang up the telephone or turn their backs on someone in the middle of a conversation. As we know, they can't bear cowardice, lies and hypocrisy. They cast aside anyone with these characteristics. After a separation, they also often cast aside the partner they've separated from. How often have I heard controllers say: *"I don't want to have anything to do with him/her."*

As *controllers* are charmers, their sex life will very often be satisfying only if preceded by seduction. This explains why *controllers* love falling in love; they love the passionate side of a relationship. When the passion begins to die òn their side, they find a way to make their partner leave them. That way they won't be accused of *betrayal*.

Female *controllers* often feel that men take advantage of them, and so are wary. They like making love when they feel like it, when they've decided to let themselves be seduced or when they feel like seducing their partner. Male *controllers* also like the idea to come from themselves. When *controllers* (men or women) want to make love and their partner refuses, they feel betrayed. They can't understand why their partner, who loves them, doesn't want to bond through lovemaking. A primary cause of their sexual problems is the bond they created with their parent of the opposite sex, whom they idealized so highly that no partner can meet their expectations.

145

Thus, the Oedipus complex has not been solved. I've noticed that in spite of their sexual problems, those who suffer from *betrayal* are those who most want to have a lover. They don't realize that this desire feeds their wound of *betrayal*, whether in thought or in action.

Controllers, therefore, often have a blockage at the sexual level. As you may remember, at the beginning of this chapter I said that controller types have developed strong sexual energy, but with the fears they develop over the years, they can block a large part of it. We can see that the energy is physically blocked when the pelvic area is distended. *controllers* can even go so far as completely renouncing a sex life, but will find a good reason to justify their decision.

As to diet, *controllers* generally eat fast, because they don't have time to waste. When they are absorbed by an important task, they can easily forget to eat altogether. They even say that eating isn't important for them. On the other hand, when they decide to eat, they'll eat a lot and will enjoy their food. They can even lose control and eat much more than their bodies need. Of the five types, they are the ones who will often spice and salt their food before tasting their meal. That way they're sure to have the last word concerning what they eat, just as they like to have the last word in a conversation.

Here are some of the illnesses that *controllers* commonly suffer from:

- AGORAPHOBIA, which, as for *dependents*, is partly due to their need to bond. However, the agoraphobia that *controllers* suffer from is marked more by the fear of going insane, whereas agoraphobics who wear the *dependent* mask more commonly fear death. I would like to point out that doctors often diagnose agoraphobia as spasmophilia. (For the definition of agoraphobia, refer to page 67)

- *Controllers* attract illnesses linked to control, to stiffness, such as all problems linked to the ARTICULATIONS or JOINTS in the body, especially the KNEES.

- They are the most prone to illnesses where you lose control of certain parts of the body, such as HEMORRHAGES, IMPOTENCE, DIARRHEA, etc.

- If they find themselves in a situation where they are totally powerless, they may be afflicted by PARALYSIS.

- They frequently have problems with their DIGESTIVE SYSTEM, especially the LIVER and the STOMACH.

- They are also more likely than others to suffer from illnesses ending in "ITIS." You will find more details in the book Your body says: Love yourself! wherein I explain that these illnesses are mainly found in people who are impatient, angry and frustrated because of their high expectations.

- *Controllers* also frequently suffer from MOUTH SORES, an affection that appears when they accuse, consciously or sub-consciously, the opposite sex of being disgusting. It's also a means of control, to avoid having to kiss.

The above-mentioned complaints and illnesses can also occur in people suffering from the other wounds, but they seem to be much more common in those suffering from *betrayal*.

It's important to realize that your parent of the opposite sex with whom you live out this wound, has suffered and probably still suffers from the same wound with his or her parent of the opposite sex. If your parents are alive, there's nothing preventing you from speaking to them about it. Listening to our parents speak about their lives with *their* parents when they were young is often a very enriching experience.

You must remember that the main reason for the presence of any wound comes from our inability to forgive ourselves for what we do to ourselves or what we do to others. It's difficult to forgive ourselves because we generally can't even see that we blame ourselves. The greater the wound of *betrayal*, the more we betray others or betray ourselves by not trusting ourselves or by breaking the promises we make to ourselves. We blame others for everything we do ourselves but don't want to see. That's why we attract people who show us what we do.

Another way to realize when we betray others or ourselves is to feel shame. Every time we want to hide our behavior (or ourselves) it's because we feel ashamed. It's normal to find it shameful that our behavior is the same as the behavior we criticize in others. We really don't want them to find out that we act the same way they do.

Remember, the characteristics and the behavior described in this chapter exist only when we decide to wear our controller mask, believing that's how we'll avoid suffering from betrayal. Depending on the depth of the wound, this mask can be worn almost never or almost always.

The distinctive behavior of *controllers* is dictated by the fear of once again experiencing the wound of *betrayal*. Each of the wounds described in this book has its respective inner behavior and attitudes. The thinking, feeling, speaking and acting that are linked to each wound show a reaction to what's happening in life. When we are reacting we are not centered, not in our hearts, and can't be happy. That's why it's so useful to be aware of those times when we are being ourselves and when we're reacting. When we become aware, we can become master of our lives instead of being controlled by our fears.

The aim of this chapter is to help you become familiar with the wound of *betrayal*. If you see yourself in the description of the *controller* mask, the last chapter contains all the information you'll need to heal this wound and to once again become your true self, without believing that the world is filled with *betrayal*. If you don't see yourself in this description, I suggest you check with those who know you well to see if they agree with you before eliminating the possibility. As I've mentioned, it is possible to have a relatively small wound of *betrayal*, in which case you may have only a few of the characteristics. You may well recognize yourself in some of the behavior patterns but not in everything I've described. It's almost impossible for one person to recognize themselves in all that I've mentioned. Remember that it is important to go by the physical descriptions first because we can easily lie to ourselves, but the physical body never lies.

If you recognize people around you as suffering from this wound, you mustn't try to change them. Try to use what you learn in this book to develop more compassion and better understand their reactive behavior. It would be better that they read this book themselves, if they show an interest, rather than trying to explain the contents in your words.

Characteristics of the wound of BETRAYAL

The awakening of the wound: Between two and four years old with the parent of the opposite sex. Breach of trust or unfulfilled expectations in their love/sexual connection. Manipulation.

Mask: Controller.

Body: Exudes strength and power. For men, shoulders wider than hips. For women, hips wider than shoulders. Protruding chest. Protruding stomach.

Eyes: Intense, seductive look. Eyes that see everything quickly.

Vocabulary: "Dissociated" "I'm able/capable" "Let me do it by myself" "I knew it" "Trust me" "I don't trust him" "Do you understand?"

Character: Believe they're responsible and strong. Want to be special and important. Don't keep their promises and their commitments or force themselves to keep them. Lie easily. Manipulating. Charmers. Have great expectations. Moody. Convinced they're right and try to convince others. Impatient. Intolerant. Understand and act fast. Perform to be noticed. Comedian. Don't confide easily. Don't show their vulnerability. Skeptical. Fear broken commitments.

Greatest fear: Dissociation, separation, being cast aside.

Eating habits: Good appetite. Eat fast. Add salt and spices. Can control themselves when busy but then lose control.

Possible illnesses: Illnesses linked to control and loss of control, agoraphobia, spasmophilia, digestive system, illnesses ending in "itis," mouth sores.

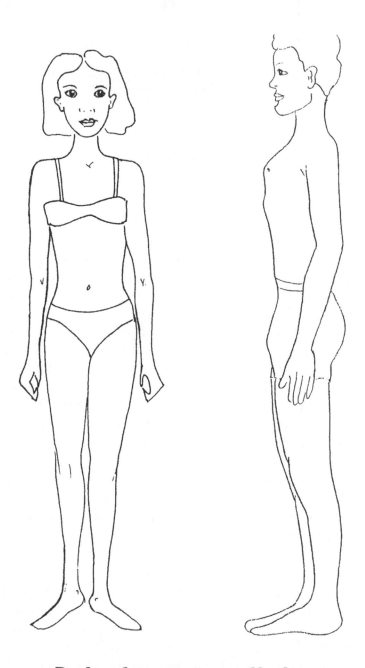

**Body of a person suffering
from the wound of INJUSTICE
(Mask of Rigidity)**

Chapter 6

Injustice

Justice is defined as the appreciation, acknowledgment and respect of the rights and merit of any individual. Synonyms of the word "just" include: upright, equitable, impartial, with integrity. *Injustice,* as you know, is the opposite of justice. We suffer from *injustice*, therefore, when we feel we aren't appreciated at our true value, when we don't feel respected, or when we don't believe we receive what we deserve. We can also suffer from *injustice* if we receive *more* than we feel we deserve. We can experience the wound of *injustice*, therefore, when we think we have more material belongings than we deserve, or on the contrary, that we don't have enough.

This wound is awakened when we are developing our individuality, that is, roughly between the ages of three and five, when we become conscious that we are human beings, complete entities, with individual differences.

As children, we find it unjust that we can't integrate our individuality; we can't express ourselves and we can't *be* ourselves. We live out this wound primarily with our parent of the same sex. If that parent is unable to feel and to express their feelings, we suffer from that parent's coldness. I'm not saying that all parents of those who suffer from injustice are cold, but that's how we, as children, perceive them. We also suffer from our parent's authoritarianism, frequent criticisms, strictness, intolerance or their conformism. In most cases, the parent concerned also suffers from the wound of injustice. It may not be lived out in the same way or under the same circumstances, but it's there and the child feels it.

People suffering from *injustice* have often told me that their relationship with their parent of the same sex was good when they were teenagers and that they were even friends with that parent. On the other hand, it was a superficial relationship, where neither the parent nor the child spoke of their true feelings.

The souls that come to Earth to heal the wound of *injustice* choose parents who will help them come into contact with their wound. One of the parents, or even both, will suffer from the same wound. When faced with *injustice*, people's reactions are to cut themselves off from their feelings, thus believing that they're protecting themselves. Even if we cut ourselves off from our feelings, that doesn't mean we don't feel anything. We create the mask of RIGIDITY to protect ourselves from this wound.

Rigid people are very sensitive, but they develop the capacity to bury their sensitivity and hide it from others. They act as if nothing touches them. That's why, if we are wearing the mask of *rigidity*, we often seem to be cold and insensitive. Of the five wounds, *rigid* people tend to cross their arms more often than others. This action blocks the area of the solar plexus so they won't feel. Another way to avoid feeling is to dress in black because that color makes it difficult to let anything through. I mentioned earlier that *withdrawers* also like to dress in black, but for a different reason; they want to disappear. Those who suffer both from *rejection* and *injustice* generally wear only black or very dark colors.

Rigid people seek justice and fairness above all. They are often perfectionists, believing that if what they say or do is perfect, it will automatically be fair. It's very difficult for them to understand that they're acting according to *their* definition of perfection, and they may still be unfair.

Those who suffer from *injustice* are inclined to envy those who have more and who, according to them, don't deserve it. They may also believe that others envy them when *they* have more. *Dependents* or *controllers* have a greater tendency to feel jealousy, which is different to envy. *Dependents* are jealous because they're afraid of being abandoned, whereas *controllers* are jealous because of their fear of *betrayal*.

The mask of *rigidity* is distinguishable by a straight, rigid body that is as perfect as possible. The body is well proportioned, with straight shoulders that are as wide as the hips. *Rigid* people may put on weight, but their bodies will continue to be well proportioned. The reason why they might gain weight is explained in the previous chapter.

I must say though, that of all the types, *rigid* people most fear gaining weight. They'll do anything to make sure they don't get fat and they really don't like having a fat stomach. When they're standing up, they often pull in their stomachs. *Rigid* women would be better off accepting that it isn't natural for women to have a perfectly flat stomach. A woman's body naturally has curves; it's part of being female.

Both *rigid* men and *rigid* women often have a nice round bottom. The women have a small waist; they like clothes that are fitted at the waist, and often wear a belt. They believe, unconsciously, that if the waist is tightly belted (in the area of the solar plexus - the region of emotions), they'll feel less.

These are lively, dynamic people. They have clear skin and bright, lively eyes. Their movements, however, are rigid, with little flexibility, which shows that they are fairly closed. An example being people whose arms don't leave their sides. Their jaws are often clenched and their necks are stiff, proudly held upright, and you can often see their veins sticking out.

If you have all the above physical characteristics, it's a sign that you suffer from a large wound of *injustice*. If you have only a few of the characteristics, your wound is less deep.

Even when young, *rigid* people realize that they are more appreciated for what they do than for what they are. Even if this isn't true, they're convinced it is. That's why they become good performers and start managing on their own, fast. They do everything to avoid problems and even when they're in the middle of one, they prefer to say that everything's fine, so they don't feel the suffering that's linked to their problem. *Rigid* people are very optimistic, often too much so. They believe that by regularly saying: *"No problem"*, problems will go away. Moreover, they do everything to solve problems themselves. They ask for help only if it becomes absolutely necessary.

When *rigid* people are disappointed or when unexpected events occur, they continue to say: *"No problem."* They manage very well to hide what they're feeling, from themselves and from others, and appear imperturbable.

Rigid people, like *controllers*, often feel they lack time, but for a different reason. *Rigid* people don't have enough time because they want everything to be perfect, whereas *controllers* don't have enough time because they're too busy worrying about other people's problems. *Rigid* people don't like being late either, but often are, because they take too long to get ready.

When *rigid* people are dealing with authority or with those who believe they're an authority on a subject, and they're convinced they're right, they'll justify their position until the "authority" agrees. They fear authority because as children they were taught that authorities were always right. When others seem to doubt them and ask a lot of questions, *rigid* people feel they're being put through an *unjust* inquisition, because they believe that they were honest and fair.

As they're always seeking justice, *rigid* people want to be sure that they deserve what they receive. Merit is important to *rigid* people. In their eyes, to merit is to obtain a reward for a good performance. If they receive something without having worked for it, they don't feel they deserve it and may end up losing what they received. Those who are extremely rigid even manage to receive nothing, because in their opinions, they have to be extraordinary to deserve a reward.

When they provide explanations, *rigid* people want all the details to be exact, but the expressions they use are far from exact, because they exaggerate so easily. They regularly use the words: *always, never* and *very.* For example, a rigid woman who says to her husband: *"You're NEVER here, you're ALWAYS away!"* doesn't realize that she's not being fair because, of course, situations that *always* or *never* occur are few and far between. For *rigid* people, everything is often *very good, very well, very special etc.* They don't, however, like others to use these words. When they do, they accuse them of exaggeration.

Religion has more impact or influence on *rigid* people than on those who suffer from the other wounds. Good and bad, right and wrong are very important for them. It's what governs their lives. This becomes obvious when we listen to the way they speak. They often start sentences with *well* or *right* to make sure that what they're going to say will be good and fair. They end their sentences with *"do you agree?"* to check their accuracy. They use lots of words that finish in *ly* like *exactly, surely, probably,* etc. They also often say: *"It's not clear."* They like clear, precise explanations.

When *rigid* people are moved or emotional, they don't want to show their feelings, but their tone of voice, which becomes dry and abrupt, betrays them. They may also laugh to hide their sensitivity and emotions. They can easily laugh for no reason, at something that others don't find funny.

When you ask *rigid* people how they are, they systematically reply: *"Very well!"* They answer very quickly because they don't want to take the time to feel. Then, during the conversation, they'll speak about several events in their lives that are not going too well. If you say to them: *"I thought you said that everything was fine!"* they'll say that they're not real problems.

Rigid people have a great fear of making mistakes. During my workshops, only *rigid* people ask: *"Did I do this exercise correctly?"* Rather than concentrating on what they feel and on what they can learn about themselves through the exercise, they're more interested in knowing if they did it well. I've also noticed that when I speak of types of behavior or attitudes, *rigid* people see them as new shortcomings, in other words they consider that it's not right to behave in such a way and they interrupt me before I've even finished to ask: *"Now what do we do with that?"* They want to have pointers on how to become perfect, fast. If they're not perfect, they have to control themselves so that the failing they've just discovered doesn't show. They don't realize that, once again, they're asking too much of themselves. *Rigid* people would like to solve everything straight away, so they don't take the time to see how they feel in a situation, to allow themselves to be human with ongoing problems to solve.

I've noticed that people with the mask of *rigidity* tend to blush easily when they're telling me something and judge themselves as *not being right*. This can happen, for example, when they tell me how hard it is for them to forgive someone who has hurt them, or when they're speaking badly about someone because they find the other person's attitude unfair. The blush shows that they're feeling ashamed of what they are or are not doing. They, however, don't know that's why they blush and sometimes they don't even realize that they're doing it. In fact, *withdrawers* and *rigid* people are those who have the greatest problems with their skin.

Because they're afraid to make mistakes, *rigid* people often find themselves in situations where they have to make choices. The more frightened we are, the more we attract situations that correspond to our fear. For example, if we want to buy something but are short of money, we will have to make a choice. We wonder if we should buy it and so have to decide whether or not to make that purchase. *Rigid* people often choose to treat themselves, but then feel that they've missed out on something else. Let's take, for example, a man who decides to treat himself to a nice holiday. Later, he thinks that he should have used that money to fix up his house. Fear of making the wrong decision often makes *rigid* people doubt themselves once their choice has been made. They constantly wonder if they made the "right" choice; if their choice was the fairest.

If you want something to be equally shared among several people, such as a cake, a bottle of wine, the bill at the restaurant, etc. you can be sure that the best person for this task is someone *rigid*. When we have group meals in restaurants, for example, I enjoy watching what happens when the bill arrives. *Controllers* take the situation in hand, saying: *"How about splitting the bill? It'll be a lot faster and less complicated."* They express themselves with so much force and control, that the others politely agree. They rapidly calculate the amount everyone has to pay by dividing the total amount by the number of people present, and then announce how much each person has to pay. That's when the *rigid* people react. They're not happy. The ones who have to pay for more than they ate don't think it's fair and the ones who ordered more expensive dishes to treat themselves don't think it fair that others should pay for it. When this situation arises, we have to start adding all over.

Rigid people are very demanding of themselves in most areas of their lives. They have a large capacity for taking on tasks and controlling themselves. In the previous chapter, we saw that *controllers* like to control what's going on around them. *Rigid* people, however, seek perfection to such a point that they are more likely to control themselves. They ask so much of themselves that others also ask a lot of them. How many times have I heard *rigid* women say to their close ones: *"Stop taking me for the bionic woman who can do everything!"* In fact, these women are speaking to *themselves*. The others are only there to reflect how much they ask of themselves.

A participant once told us how his father used to say to him: *"You have no rights, only duties."* This phrase has remained with him ever since his tender years and he admits to having problems letting himself go. He doesn't allow himself to stop, to have fun, to rest. He feels that he must always be productive. He has to do his duty. As there is always *something* to be done in our daily lives, *rigid*

163

people rarely allow themselves to relax without feeling guilty. They justify relaxing or having fun by saying, for example, that they deserve it after all they've done. Moreover, *rigid* people feel particularly guilty if they do nothing while someone else is working. They find that unfair. That's why their bodies, particularly their legs and arms are tensed even when they're resting. They have to make an effort to loosen up and relax their legs. I only realized this myself a few years ago. When I'm sitting at the hairdresser's or reading, I suddenly realize how tense my legs are, even though I'm relaxed. I have to make a conscious effort to relax my legs, my shoulders or my arms.

Rigid people also find it hard, not only to respect their limits, but also to know when they have reached them. As they don't take the time to feel if what they're doing corresponds to their needs, they often do too much and only stop when they are on the verge of collapse. Moreover, they find it very difficult to ask for help. They prefer to do everything themselves so that it will be perfect. That's why *rigid* people are more prone to *burnout* than others.

You can see that the greatest *injustice rigid* people commit is towards themselves. They easily, blame themselves, for example, if they buy something that they feel they don't really need and don't buy things for their loved ones at the same time. To allow themselves to buy the desired article, they have to find a way to justify their purchase; they have to find a reason why they deserve it. Otherwise, they will accuse themselves of being unfair.

The wound of *injustice* is another of the wounds that I have to heal in this life. I have often lost some brand new thing, or broken it when I used it for the first time, if I thought I didn't really need or deserve it. That was how I knew I felt guilty, because on the conscious level, I was convinced that I had finished my process of acceptance and that I no longer felt guilty.

I learned that speaking to ourselves mentally and trying to convince ourselves that we deserve something isn't acceptance on our part. In this case, the missing ingredient is the ability to feel that we deserve whatever it is. We can *think* we deserve things, but we also have to be able to *feel* it, so that we can allow ourselves to buy whatever we have chosen and find it fair. Several people have heard me say that the biggest treat I can give myself is to go look in the shops and buy myself something beautiful, and especially something I don't need. Today I know that I need to do this to help me get past the belief that I must deserve, or merit, something before I can have it, and to help me allow myself to have what makes me feel good, without guilt.

I've often noticed that *rigid* type participants in my workshops like to make sure that their close ones know they're taking classes and that they're not on holiday, but are there to work on themselves. Those who come from a distance and have to book a hotel will reserve the cheapest one possible, so as not to feel guilty. Some even hide from their close ones the fact that they have to stay in a hotel just in case they would think it unfair. When *rigid* people try to hide what they do or what they buy, it's because they feel not only guilt, but shame as well.

Rigid people like those around them to know everything they've done and everything they still have to do. *Controllers* also do this, but not for the same reason. *Controllers* want to show how responsible they are, whereas *rigid* people want to show that they deserve a reward. That way, if they treat themselves to something special or to a holiday, they don't feel guilty. They also hope that those around them will find it acceptable that they "spoil" themselves. As you can see, the notion of merit is very important for *rigid* people. They don't like to be called lucky because, in their eyes, *being lucky* is not fair. They want to deserve everything that happens to them. If someone calls them lucky, they'll say: *"It's not luck; I worked really hard to get there."* If they consider they really have been lucky and that they don't deserve what they're getting, they'll feel extremely ill at ease and will feel indebted. They'll make sure that they don't keep everything for themselves.

One of the characteristics of *rigid* people that others find hard to understand is that they often find it even more unjust to be privileged in comparison to others. Because of this, some *rigid* people subconsciously act in such a way that they lose what they have received, or find a way to stop receiving more than others. Other *rigid* people find something to complain about, to hide the fact that they have more. Others feel that they, in turn, have to give. Being of the *rigid* type myself, I can confirm this, because ever since I was very small, I've always had a lot of talent and ease in several fields. I was often the teacher's pet. From an early age, I started to do a lot to help others so that it would be fair, because I found it unfair to have more than they did. In fact, this is often the reason why *rigid* people want to help others.

It is, therefore, not surprising to learn that *rigid* people also have difficulty receiving presents because they then feel indebted. Rather than feeling that they have to give the other person something of the same value (to be fair), they prefer not to receive anything and they refuse the gift. When someone offers to pay for their meal, for example, they prefer to decline rather than to have to remember that the next time, it'll be their turn to pay. If they accept, they promise themselves that, *to be fair*, the next time will be on them.

It's normal that those who suffer from *injustice* attract situations that, according to them, are unjust, more often than others. However, those who don't suffer from this wound interpret differently the situations that *rigid* people qualify as being unjust. Here's an example: Not long ago, I was speaking with a woman who was the eldest in her family. She had always thought it unfair to be the eldest because she had to look after the other children and above all, had to be an example for them. Other women, on the other hand, have told me that they found it unfair that they were the second or third in line, because they rarely had new clothes (wearing the hand-me-downs from the eldest), and because the eldest often manipulated them.

How often I have heard *rigid* men and women say that they found it unfair that they had to look after their old, ill parents. What they really found unfair was that their brothers and sisters had lots of good excuses for not

167

looking after them, which meant that they had no choice in the matter. This situation doesn't happen by chance. Our wound of *injustice* attracts these situations and this will only stop when the wound is healed.

I spoke earlier of *rigid* people's capacity to control themselves and create obligations for themselves. It's the rigid part of us that manages to follow a diet. People who don't suffer from the wound of *injustice*, who aren't at all *rigid*, won't manage to stay on a diet, because they won't be able to control themselves the way *rigid* people do. *Rigid* people don't understand why *masochists* don't go on diets. They can't accept this. They believe that, if they really wanted to, others could manage to control themselves as they do. Remember, *rigid* people's motivation for creating obligations for themselves is to reach perfection, according to their ideal.

Non-*rigid* people will accuse themselves of lacking willpower; it is important, however, to see the difference between willpower and control. People who control themselves are people who impose things upon themselves even if those things don't correspond to their needs. It goes without saying that behind control hides fear. People with willpower know what they want and are determined to obtain it. They succeed by structuring themselves, never losing sight of their objectives and at the same time, respecting their needs and their limits. When an event thwarts their plans, they know how to be flexible and are capable of drawing up new plans to reach their objectives. *Rigid* people don't even take the time to see if their desire really corresponds to their needs. They don't take the time to internalize and to ask themselves: *"How do I feel with this desire and with the means I've chosen to obtain it?"*

Rigid people also find it very hard to see the difference between rigidity and discipline. Here is my favorite definition of rigidity: *rigid* people forget their initial need and concentrate more on the means they have chosen to satisfy that need. Disciplined people find the means to satisfy their need without ever losing sight of their need. An example: someone decides to walk one hour a day to be in better health and in better physical condition. The means is, therefore, walking. *Rigid* people force themselves to walk every day, irrespective of the weather or of how they're feeling. If, one day, they don't go, they feel bad. Disciplined people don't forget why they walk every day. Some days, they may decide not to go, knowing that it's better for their health. Forcing themselves would bring them more harm than good. They don't feel guilty; they start again the next day with a clear conscience. Disciplined people don't abandon a project because they missed out on one or two days or because there was a change in their schedule.

Rigid people may sometimes intervene in a situation, but it's not to control and attract attention or to demonstrate their strength, as is the case for *controllers*. *Rigid* people only intervene if what has just been said seems unfair. They rectify what has been said, whereas *controllers* add to what has been said. *Rigid* people may reproach others if they sincerely believe that those people could have accomplished their tasks better with the abilities and the talent they have. *Controllers*, however, will reproach others if the tasks haven't been done their way, if they're not in line with their tastes or expectations.

Another difference between the way *rigid* people control and the way *controllers* control, is that *rigid* people control themselves so they won't seem unfair to the other person. *Controllers*, on the other hand, control themselves in order to control situations or other people more efficiently and to show that they're the strongest.

Rigid people like everything to be tidy. They don't like having to look for things. Some even become obsessed with their need for everything to be perfectly tidy.

Rigid people are also very stressed because everything they do has to be perfect. *Controllers* too are stressed, but for a different reason: they want to succeed. They want to avoid failure at all costs because they're worried about their image and don't want their reputation to be affected.

People with a *rigidity* mask are rarely ill. In any case, even if they are suffering from something, they only begin to feel it once it becomes serious. They are very hard on their bodies. They can bang themselves somewhere, have a big bruise, and not feel anything. If they feel a little pain when they hurt themselves, their control mechanism, which gives them an enormous faculty to shut out the pain, is immediately triggered. In films or in thrillers where people are being tortured, notice that the actors who are chosen always have the physical characteristics of *rigid* people.

A policeman is always recognizable, in films or in life, because of his rigid body. Policemen may also have other wounds, but their *rigid* part chooses the career where they believe they are bringing *justice* to Earth. If, however, a policeman or a spy seems to enjoy showing his power and strength, it's his *controller* mask that will have made him choose this job.

I've often noticed that *rigid* people boast about the fact that they *never* need medicine or a doctor. Many of them don't even have a family doctor and if an emergency occurred, they wouldn't know where to turn. When they decide to ask for help, you can be sure that they must have been suffering for a long time and have reached their limit in self-control. They haven't managed to feel the part of them that has decided: *"I won't feel."* It therefore takes longer for them to know they have reached their limit in suffering.

It's important to know that we can't control ourselves all our lives. We all have physical, emotional and mental limits. That's why we often hear others say of *rigid* people: *"I don't understand what's happened to them. They never used to get ill and now, it's one thing after another."* This situation arises when *rigid* people can no longer control themselves.

The most common emotion felt by *rigid* people is anger, especially towards themselves. When they're angry, however, their first reaction is to attack someone else. They are, in fact, angry with themselves when they don't do the right thing. Let's take the case of a *rigid* person who lends money to a friend knowing that the friend in ques-

171

tion often has money problems. She lends him the money because he has promised to pay her back in two weeks when he's expecting to receive some money. He doesn't, however, keep his promise. The *rigid* person will be angry with herself because she wasn't right in giving him another chance. They often want to give chances to others; they believe its *fair*. If they're very rigid, it's highly likely that they don't even want to see their anger and they'll try to smooth over the situation by excusing the other.

This same example can be felt as *betrayal*, if it's a *controller* who's lending the money. He, however, won't feel angry with himself like the *rigid* person does. He'll feel angry with the friend he trusted, for not having kept his word and for not having paid him back.

Rigid people also have problems showing and receiving love. They often think too late of what they would have liked to say, or of the affection they would have liked to show to those they love. They often promise themselves that the next time they see their loved ones, they'll tell them, but when the time comes, they forget or they can't. They are, therefore, often seen as cold and unaffectionate. They may seem unfair to others, but above all, they are unfair to themselves because they deprive themselves of expressing what they really feel.

Rigid people, being very sensitive, avoid letting themselves be touched psychologically by others. This fear of being touched or affected by other people can be strong enough that they create skin problems for themselves. Because the skin is a contact organ, it helps us to touch or to be touched by others. If the skin is repulsive, it will, therefore, distance others. People who have skin problems are generally ashamed of what others might think of them.

This fear of being touched by others can be seen in the closed posture of *rigid* people. Arms stuck to the body, especially from the shoulders to the elbows; hands and legs closed; one leg sticking to the other - are all indications that they close themselves off.

Rigid people use comparison to be unfair to themselves. They often compare themselves to those they consider better and above all more perfect than they are. Putting themselves down like that is a serious *injustice* and a form of *rejection* of their being. It's very common for *rigid* people to feel they were compared, either with their brothers and sisters or with their friends or peers, when they were young. At that time, they accused their parents of being unfair because they didn't know that their parents were showing them what they were doing to themselves internally.

If you recognize yourself as suffering from the wound of *injustice* and wearing the mask of *rigidity*, the first thing to do is to admit how often in one day you are unfair to others and especially to yourself. It's the hardest part to admit, but it is the beginning of your healing process. In the next chapter, we will go into ways to heal this wound.

I remember an incident with one of my sons, who was 17 at the time, which really touched upon the wound of *injustice* that I'm healing in this life. One day, when we were alone, I asked him: *"Tell me which of my attitudes as a mother has made you suffer the most since you were little?"* He replied: *"Your injustice!"* I was flabbergasted. I was so surprised that I couldn't even speak. I remembered all the situations where I had tried to be a fair mother. Putting myself in my children's shoes, I can now understand that they found some of my acts and attitudes unfair. However, the physical characteristics of my son indicate that the experiences of *injustice* that he lived with me awakened his wound of *betrayal*. It's true that he must have found unfair his father's indifference in regards to my *injustice* towards him. In his body we can see two wounds, the wound of *injustice* and the wound of *betrayal*. This is fairly common. It means that one has something to solve with each of his parents: the wound of *betrayal* with the parent of the opposite sex and the wound of *injustice* with the parent of the same sex.

Rigid people's greatest fear is coldness. They have as much difficulty accepting their own coldness as they do accepting that of others. They do everything possible to display warmth. Moreover, they believe that they *are* warm and don't realize that others may find them cold and insensitive. They don't realize that they avoid feeling their sensitivity because they don't want to show their vulnerability. They can't accept that they're cold because that would mean being *heartless*, which boils down to being *unjust*. That's why it's so important for *rigid* people to hear that they're good, that is to say, *good in what they do* and *good people*. In the first case, they consider themselves perfect and in the second they consider themselves warm. They also have difficulties in accepting other people's coldness. If someone is cold towards them, their hearts ache and they immediately wonder what it is that they said or did that wasn't right and that incited the other person to act that way towards them.

Rigid people are attracted by anything noble. Respect and honor are equally important. People with important titles easily impress them. They become even better performers if they think that they may be awarded a title, and are ready to make all the necessary effort and sacrifices to succeed, although of course, *rigid* people don't see it as sacrifice.

Rigid people generally find it hard to let themselves go and to feel pleasure in their sex lives. They find it hard to express all the tenderness they feel. They are, however, physically the sexiest looking. *Rigid* people like wearing tight fitting, sexy clothes and like being physically attractive. *Rigid* women are often *teasers*; they like attracting men but then push them away coldly if they consider that things are going too far. During their teenage years, *rigid* people are those who will hold themselves back the longest, those who will control themselves the most, wanting to keep themselves pure and perfect for the man of their dreams. They easily create an ideal of sexual relationships that is unrealistic. When they finally decide to give themselves to someone, they are usually disappointed because it doesn't match up to their ideal. When *rigid* people find it hard to commit themselves, it's because they're afraid of making a mistake in their choice of partner. This fear of commitment is different from that of *controllers* who fear commitment because they fear separation; they fear having to break their commitment.

Rigid people have several taboos in their sexual relationships because the good and the bad also govern their sex lives. *Rigid* women are particularly good at feigning orgasms. The deeper the wound, the more *rigid* the person and the more difficult it is for them to reach an orgasm. *Rigid* men may suffer from premature ejaculation or even impotence depending on their ability to enjoy themselves in life.

I've also noticed that many prostitutes have the physical characteristics of *rigid* people. They are able to have sexual relationships purely for money because they manage to cut themselves off from their feelings much more easily than other people.

Concerning diet, *rigid* people prefer salty food to sweet food. Above all they like crunchy foods. I know some that enjoy crunching ice cubes. They generally try to have a balanced diet. Of the five types, they are the ones who are most likely to become vegetarian. That doesn't necessarily mean that being a vegetarian corresponds to the needs of their bodies. Remember that *rigid* people often make decisions to be fair. If they are vegetarians because they feel that it's unfair to kill animals, for example, their organisms may suffer from a lack of protein. On the other hand, if they make this choice because they don't like meat and because, on top of that, they're happy to contribute to saving animals, the motivation isn't the same. Their bodies, in this case, will feel all the better.

If they control their diet too much, they may lose control from time to time and indulge in sweet things or in alcohol. If they do this in front of others, they are quick to explain to everybody that this never usually happens to them, that today was really an exception. When *rigid* people find themselves in a situation that touches them deeply, a birthday, a party or a special meeting, for example, they find it hard to control themselves. It's at moments like this that they may eat things they usually forbid themselves, especially things that might make them put on weight. When this happens, they justify themselves by saying: *"I NEVER eat this, but today I want to keep you company."* They seem to have completely forgotten that not long before, they had said exactly the same thing. They feel guilty, resent themselves and promise that they'll start controlling themselves again the next day.

Here are some of the complaints and illnesses that people wearing the *rigidity* mask may attract:

• They feel the rigidity in their bodies in the form of STIFFNESS or TENSION in the upper part of their BACKS or in their NECKS, as well as in the flexible parts of their bodies (ankles, knees, hips, elbows, wrists etc.) *Rigid* people like cracking their fingers to try to loosen them up. They can, therefore, feel the shell that protects their bodies but they can't feel what's hiding behind that shell.

• BURNOUT, which has already been mentioned.

• Illnesses ending in "ITIS" such as TENDINITIS, BURSITIS, ARTHRITIS. Any illness ending in "ITIS" indicates repressed inner anger and this is frequently the case for *rigid* people.

- They may also suffer from TORTICOLLIS (WRYNECK) because they have difficulties seeing all the aspects of a situation that they consider unfair.

- Problems of CONSTIPATION and HEMORRHOIDS are very frequent due to their difficulty in letting go and to the way they restrain themselves in life.

- *Rigid* people may also suffer from CRAMPS, which occur when they hang onto something or restrain themselves out of fear.

- Because they find it hard to let themselves enjoy life, they may have problems with their BLOOD CIRCULATION and may get VARICOSE VEINS.

- They frequently have problems of DRY SKIN or other SKIN PROBLEMS: They may get SPOTS or PIMPLES on their faces when they're afraid of making a mistake, of *losing face* or of not meeting their own expectations. PSORIASIS is also common among *rigid* people. They attract this ailment so that they won't feel too good and be too happy (which might be unfair to others). It's remarkable how often psoriasis appears during their holidays or when things are going really well for them.

- LIVER problems are frequent due to their repressed anger.

- NERVOUSNESS is common, even though most of the time, *rigid* people manage to control it so that it's not visible to others.

- *Rigid* people frequently suffer from INSOMNIA, especially those who feel good only when everything is finished and perfect. They think so much about everything they still have to do that they wake up and can't get back to sleep.

- They also have problems with VISION because it's hard for them to see that they've made a bad decision or that they had a bad perception of a situation. They prefer not to see anything that they consider imperfect; that way they won't suffer. They often use the expression: *"It's not clear,"* which doesn't help improve their vision.

Generally speaking, most of the illnesses that *rigid* people suffer from are not serious enough for them to see a doctor. They wait for their problems to heal themselves or they try to treat themselves alone, without telling others, because it's too hard for them to admit that they might need help. When they decide to ask for help, it may well be because the problem has become serious.

The above-mentioned complaints and illnesses can also occur in people suffering from the other wounds, but they seem to be much more common in people suffering from *injustice*.

I mentioned in the last chapter that the *controller* mask (wound of *betrayal*) hides the wound of *abandonment*. The same goes for the mask of *rigidity,* which hides the wound of *rejection*. If you refer to the chapter on *rejection*, you'll see that this wound is developed in the first few months of life, whereas the wound of *injustice* is developed between the ages of three and five. The child who feels rejected, for one reason or another, tries to be as perfect as possible, so that it won't happen again. After a few years, they don't feel that their parents love them any more, in spite of all their efforts, and they consider that unjust. They therefore decide to control themselves even more and to become so perfect that they'll never be rejected. That's how they create the mask of *rigidity*. They cut themselves off from their feelings so they will no longer feel the pain of *rejection*. When, physically, the wound of *injustice* is more pronounced than the wound of *rejection*, it's because they suffer more from *injustice* than from *rejection*. For other people, the opposite may be true.

A person may suffer from *rejection* without suffering from *injustice* but, from my observations, all people who suffer from *injustice* hide a wound of *rejection*. This explains why, as they get older, the bodies of *rigid* men and women grow smaller. Their bodies gradually take on the characteristics of the *withdrawer* mask. Medical science calls this phenomenon osteoporosis.

If you see yourself with the wound of *injustice*, it's important to realize that your parent of the same sex has suffered and probably still suffers from the same wound with his or her parent of the same sex. In the next chapter,

I explain what you need to do with this parent to help you heal your wound.

You must remember that the presence of any wound comes from our inability to forgive ourselves for what we do to ourselves or to others. It's difficult to forgive ourselves because we generally can't even see that we blame ourselves. The greater the wound of *injustice*, the more unjust we will be to other people or ourselves. We will ask too much of ourselves by not respecting our limits and not allowing ourselves to enjoy life. We blame others for everything we do ourselves but don't want to see. That's why we attract people who reflect what we are doing.

If we feel shame, it is another indication that we suffer from *injustice* or that we are being unjust to others. Every time we want to hide our behavior or ourselves it's because we feel ashamed. It's normal to find it shameful that our behavior is the same as the behavior we criticize in others. We really don't want them to find out that we act the same way they do.

> **Remember, the characteristics and the behavior described in this chapter exist only when we decide to wear our mask of rigidity, believing that's how we'll avoid suffering from injustice. Depending on the depth of the wound and the intensity of the pain, we will wear this mask almost never or almost always.**

The distinctive behavior of *rigid* people is dictated by the fear of once again experiencing the wound of *injustice*. Each of the wounds described in this book has its respective inner behavior and attitudes. The thinking, feeling, speaking and acting that are linked to each wound show a reaction to what's happening in life. When we are reacting, we are not centered, not in our hearts, and can't be happy. That's why it's so useful to be aware of when we are being ourselves and when we're reacting. When we recognize the difference, we will be able to become masters of our lives instead of letting ourselves be controlled by our fears.

The aim of this chapter is to help you to become familiar with the wound of *injustice*. If you see yourself in the description of this wound, the last chapter contains all the information you'll need to heal this wound and to once again become yourself, without believing that the world is filled with *injustice*. If you don't see yourself in this description, I suggest you check with those who know you well to see if they agree with you. It is possible your wound of *injustice* is small; in this case, you may have only a few of the characteristics. On the other hand, you may well recognize yourself in many of the behavior patterns but not in everything I've described. It's almost impossible for one person to recognize themselves in all that I've mentioned. Remember that it is important to go first by the physical description because, though we can easily lie to ourselves, the physical body never lies.

If you recognize people around you suffering from this wound, you mustn't try to change them. Try to use what you learn in this book to develop more compassion for them, to understand their reactive behavior. It would be better that they read this book themselves, if they show an interest, rather than trying to explain the contents in your words.

Characteristics of the wound of INJUSTICE

Awakening of the wound: Between three and five years old with the parent of the same sex. Must perform and be perfect. Block their individuality.

Mask: Rigidity.

Body: Straight, rigid and as perfect as possible. Well proportioned. Round bottom. Small waist marked by clothes with fitted waists or belts. Rigid movements. Clear skin. Clenched jaw. Stiff neck, held proudly.

Eyes: Bright and lively. Clear.

Vocabulary: "No problem" "Always/never" "Very good/very well" "Very special" "Precisely" "Exactly" "Surely" "Do you agree?"

Character: Perfectionist. Envious. Cut off from feelings. Often cross their arms. Perform to be perfect. Over-optimistic. Lively, dynamic. Justify themselves. Have difficulty asking for help. Can laugh for no reason to hide their sensitivity. Tone of voice is dry and abrupt. Don't admit they have problems. Doubt their choices. Compare themselves - better/worse. Have difficulty receiving in general. Find it unfair to receive less than others but even more unfair to receive more. Have difficulty in enjoying themselves without feeling guilty. Don't respect their limits, ask a lot of themselves. Rigidly control themselves. Like tidiness. Rarely ill, hard on their bodies. Quick tempered. Cold, with difficulty showing their affection. Like to look sexy.

Greatest fear: Coldness.

Eating habits: Prefer salty food to sweet. Like anything crunchy. Control their weight. Justify themselves and are ashamed when they lose control.

Possible illnesses: Burnout. Unable to reach orgasm (women). Premature ejaculation or impotence (men). Illnesses finishing in "ITIS," such as tendinitis, bursitis, arthritis, etc. Torticollis, constipation, hemorrhoids, cramps, poor blood circulation, liver problems, varicose veins, skin problems, nervousness, insomnia, bad eyesight.

Chapter 7

Healing the wounds and transforming the masks

Before describing the steps that lead to healing each type of wound and mask, I would like to share with you my observations concerning the way each type speaks, sits, dances and so on. This highlights the behavior differences that are linked to the masks.

Our voices and the way we speak differ depending on the mask we wear.

- *Withdrawers* have a feeble, dull voice.

- *Dependents* use a childlike voice with a plaintive tone.

- *Masochists* often add intonation to their voices to make them sound interested.

- *Rigid* people speak mechanically, with restraint.

- *Controllers* have a loud voice that carries.

Here is the way each character type dances.

›   *Withdrawers* don't particularly like dancing. When they do dance, they move very little, and dance discreetly so they won't be noticed. They exude: "Don't look at me too much."

›   *Dependents* prefer dances where there's physical contact, because this gives them the opportunity to cling to their partners. Sometimes they literally seem to be hanging on to the other. This says: *"Look how my partner loves me."*

›   *Masochists* love dancing and use this opportunity to express their sensuality. They dance for the pleasure of dancing. They exude: *"Look how sensual I can be."*

›   *Controllers* take up a lot of space. They like dancing, and while they're dancing, they like to seduce. It's especially an opportunity for them to be watched. Their body language is saying: *"Look at me."*

›   *Rigid* people dance very well and have good rhythm, in spite of their rigid legs. They are careful not to make mistakes. They are often people who will take dancing lessons. Very *rigid* people are serious, hold themselves straight and seem to be counting their steps as they dance. The message: *"Look how well I dance."*

What sort of car do you prefer? The following indicates which of your personalities influences your choice:

›   *Withdrawers* like dark colored cars that go unnoticed.

› *Dependents* prefer comfortable cars that are different from the norm.

› *Masochists* choose small cars where they are squashed.

› *Controllers* buy powerful cars that will be noticed.

› *Rigid* people prefer classic, high-performance cars because they want to get their money's worth.

You can apply these characteristics to other personal preferences, such as clothes.

The way we sit shows what's happening to us while we're speaking or listening.

› *Withdrawers* tend to disappear into their chairs and love hiding their feet under their legs. When not connected to the earth, they can withdraw much more easily.

› *Dependents* lounge in their chairs or lean on something, such as the arm of the chair, for example. They hunch the top of their backs forward.

› *Masochists* sit with their legs apart. As they very often choose a chair that isn't made for them, they look uncomfortable.

› *Controllers* lean backwards with their arms folded when they are listening. When they speak, they lean forward to be more convincing.

> › *Rigid* people sit up straight. They can go as far as pressing their legs together and keeping them in line with their bodies, which accentuates their rigid aspect. When they cross their arms and legs, it's so they won't feel what's going on.

I've noticed that people can change the way they sit several times during an interview, depending on what's going on inside them. For example, a woman suffering from the wound of *abandonment* and *injustice* spoke to me about the problems in her life. While she was speaking, her body went limp and the top of her back slumped; she was in her wound of *abandonment*. A few minutes later, when I asked her a question about something she didn't want to touch on, her body became straight and rigid and she denied any problems in that area. We can also change the way we speak several times during a single conversation.

I could give you many other examples; however, in the coming months, I'm sure you'll begin to recognize when you or someone around you is wearing a mask, by observing their physical and psychological attitudes and your own. You'll know what fear is prompting the action.

I've also observed a very interesting fact concerning fear. While reading this book, you'll notice that I speak about the greatest fear felt by each character type. I've observed that people wearing a particular mask don't recognize their fear, but the people around them can easily see what it is that they want to avoid at all costs.

› *Withdrawers'* greatest fear is panic. They don't realize this because they often disappear just before panic sets in. On the other hand, those close to them recognize their panic because most of the time, the panic in their eyes gives them away.

› *Dependents'* greatest fear is solitude. They don't see this because they make sure that they are rarely alone. When they are alone, they can convince themselves that they're happy and don't realize that they feverishly look for things to do to pass the time. When they are physically alone, the television and the telephone keep them company. It's easier for their close ones to see and especially to feel their great fear of solitude, which is with them even when they're surrounded by others, because their sad eyes betray them.

› *Masochists'* greatest fear is freedom. They don't believe they're free and don't *feel* free because of all the constraints and obligations they've created. Those around them, on the other hand, consider them to be extremely free because they generally find the way and the time to do what they want to do. They don't wait for the agreement of others before making decisions. Even if what they decide prevents them from being free, in the eyes of others, they had all the freedom in the world to decide otherwise, had they wanted to. Their big eyes that are open to the world show us their great interest in everything and their desire to experiment with different things.

> *Controllers'* greatest fear is dissociation and being cast aside. They don't see to what point they create conflict or problems that provide a reason to stop speaking to someone. Even though they attract separation or situations where they cast people aside, they don't see that this is what they are afraid of. On the contrary, they try to profess that these separations are better for them. They believe that in this way, they'll no longer be "had." The fact that they're very sociable and can easily make new acquaintances prevents them from seeing how many people in their lives they have cast aside. Those who are close to them realize this more easily. Their eyes also betray them. When they are angry, their eyes become hard and even frightening to the point that they distance others.

> *Rigid* people's greatest fear is coldness. They have difficulty recognizing their own coldness because they consider themselves to be warm people who do their utmost to make everything around them fair and harmonious. They are also generally faithful to their friends. On the other hand, those who are close to them often see this coldness, not only in their eyes, but also in their dry, stiff attitude, which is especially visible when they feel unjustly accused.

~~~~~~~~~~~~~~~~~

The first step toward healing a wound consists in RECOGNIZING and ACCEPTING it, without necessarily agreeing that it's there. Accepting means looking at it, observing it, knowing that having things to solve is part of the human experience. We aren't bad people because something can still hurt us.

Creating a mask to protect yourself was a heroic act, an act of love toward yourself. This mask helped you to survive and to adapt to the family environment that you chose for this lifetime.

The real reason we are born into a family or are attracted to others suffering from the same wounds is that, at the beginning, when we find others to be the same as we are, we don't feel we are so bad. After a while, when we begin to see failings in others, we no longer accept them as they are. We then try to change them, not realizing that what we don't accept in them are parts of ourselves we don't want to see, for fear of having to change. We think that we have to change, when in fact we have to be healed. That's why it's so important to recognize our wounds, that way we can heal, rather than change, ourselves.

Remember that each of these wounds ensues from an accumulation of experiences that are spread out over several past lives. It is, therefore, absolutely normal that it's difficult for us to face them again in this life. Since we haven't managed to face our wounds in past lives, we can't expect to be able to face them in this life simply by saying: *"I want to be healed."* On the other hand, by deciding to heal our wounds, we are taking the first steps toward feeling compassion, patience and tolerance for ourselves. We will simultaneously develop these attitudes toward others.

These qualities are gifts that your journey towards being healed will bring you. I'm sure that when reading the previous chapters, you discovered the wounds of your loved ones. This may help you more easily understand their behavior and so to feel greater tolerance towards them.

As we've said, it's important not to take the literal sense of the words used to identify the wounds or masks. We can, for example, be rejected in life, but feel we've been betrayed, abandoned, humiliated or feel that *injustice* was done. Someone may be unfair with us and we might feel rejected, humiliated, betrayed or abandoned. As you can see, *it's not the experience that counts, but what we feel when going through that experience.* That's why it's so important to refer to the description of the physical characteristics of a wound before referring to the behavioral characteristics, in order to recognize our wounds. The body never lies. It always reflects what's happening on the emotional and mental planes. I suggest you read the physical description of each wound several times so that you grasp the differences between them.

I know that more and more people turn to plastic surgery to correct certain aspects of their physical body. In my opinion, they are tricking themselves. Just because they are no longer able to see the physical aspects of a wound in their body doesn't mean that the wound itself is healed. Several people who have had plastic surgery have told me they were disappointed that whatever it was they wanted to hide or to remove, reappeared after two or three years. This is why surgeons who specialize in plastic surgery never guarantee that the result will last for life. On the other hand, if you decide, out of love for yourself, to take your physical body in hand through plastic surgery, while remaining conscious of your wounds and working on yourself on the emotional, mental and spiritual levels, then there is a great chance that the plastic surgery will be beneficial and that your body will accept it.

Some people try to fool themselves on the physical level, but there are many more who fool themselves on the behavioral level; in other words, on the level of their inner attitudes. This often happens in the workshop *Characters and Wounds* where I explain the wounds in detail. Some participants see themselves completely in the description of the behavior patterns of one particular type, whereas their bodies are showing another type altogether.

I remember a young man in his early thirties who told me that ever since he had been a little boy he had experienced *rejection*. He suffered from not having a stable relationship. According to him, the reason for this was the numerous occasions on which he had been rejected. After a little while, I said to him: *"Are you sure that you feel rejected, or do you rather feel that it's a great injustice?"* I then explained to him that his body showed signs of a wound of *injustice*. He was very surprised. I suggested he take time to think about it. When I saw him the following week, he was all excited saying that in the past week he had understood and shed light on a lot of things. He had finally come into contact with his wound of *injustice*.

This behavior is not surprising. The ego does everything to prevent us from seeing our wounds; it's convinced that if we touch upon them, we won't be able to deal with the pain linked to these wounds. It's the ego that convinced us to create our masks to avoid the suffering.

The ego always believes it's taking the easiest path, but in fact, it complicates our lives. When intelligence governs our lives, it is at first difficult because we have to make an effort, but in the end, it simplifies our lives tremendously.

The longer we wait to heal our wounds, the deeper they become. Each time we go through a situation that awakens and touches upon a wound, we add another layer. It's like a physical wound that spreads. The worse it gets, the more afraid we are to touch it. It becomes a vicious cycle. It can even become a form of obsession; in other words, we can end up believing that the world is there to make us suffer. For example, a very *rigid* person will see *injustice* everywhere and will become an excessive perfectionist. W*ithdrawers* will feel rejected by everyone and will convince themselves that no one could ever love them.

The advantage to discovering our wounds is that we are finally looking in the right place. Until we do, we are like someone whose doctor treats them for liver problems when in fact, they have heart problems. This situation can go on for years, as with the young man who tried to find a solution to the *rejection* he thought he was suffering from, so nothing was solved. After having touched on what *really* upset him, he was able to set about healing his wound.

I would like to specify that there is a difference between having the *dependent* mask and suffering from affective dependency. Not only those who suffer from the wound of abandonment (and who, therefore, wear the *dependent* mask), suffer from a lack of affection. We can all, irrespective of our wounds, be dependent on the affective level. Why? Because we become affectively dependent when we lack affection, and we lack affection when we don't love ourselves enough. We, therefore, look to others for love to try to convince ourselves that we are lovable. Each mask is precisely there to show us that we stop ourselves from being who we are because we don't love ourselves enough. Remember that all the behavior patterns associated with each of the masks are *reactions* and not behavior patterns based on the love we have for ourselves. The *dependent*, on the other hand, requires more attention. He never has enough to his liking.

Before going any farther, it's important to the healing process that we understand the explanations contained in the last five chapters concerning the parent with whom each of the wounds is generally lived out. Let's recap:

- *REJECTION* IS LIVED OUT WITH THE PARENT OF THE SAME SEX. *Withdrawers* therefore feel rejected by those of the same sex. They accuse them of rejecting them and feel more anger towards others than towards themselves. When, on the other hand, they feel rejected by someone of the opposite sex, they feel more anger toward, and so reject, *themselves*. It is also highly likely that what they consider to be *rejection* in the case of people of the opposite sex is, in fact, *abandonment*.

- *ABANDONMENT* IS LIVED OUT WITH THE PARENT OF THE OPPOSITE SEX. *Dependents* easily feel abandoned by those of the opposite sex and will accuse them rather than themselves. When they experience abandonment with someone of the same sex, they accuse themselves, believing that they didn't give the other person enough attention or the attention they needed. What they believe to be an experience of abandonment with people of the same sex is often rejection.

⊚ *HUMILIATION* IS OFTEN LIVED OUT WITH THE MOTHER, whether we are a man or a woman. *Masochists,* therefore, easily feel humiliated by the female sex. They tend to accuse them. If they experience *humiliation* with a male, they accuse themselves and feel ashamed of their behavior or their thoughts regarding the other person. This wound can be lived out with the father if he was the one who attended to the physical needs of the child, if he taught the child to be clean, to eat alone, to dress themselves, etc. If this is the case for you, invert what has just been said concerning the male and female sexes.

⊚ *BETRAYAL* IS LIVED OUT WITH THE PARENT OF THE OPPOSITE SEX. *Controllers,* therefore, easily feel betrayed by people of the opposite sex and blame them for their pain and their emotions. When they experience *betrayal* with someone of the same sex, they will rather blame and resent themselves for not having seen the experience coming in time to prevent it. It's probable that what they call *betrayal*, on the part of people of the same sex, is in fact an experience that activates their wound of *injustice*.

◉ *INJUSTICE* IS LIVED OUT WITH THE PARENT OF THE SAME SEX. *Rigid* people, therefore, suffer from *injustice* with people of the same sex and accuse them of being unfair towards them. If they go through an experience that they consider to be unfair with someone of the opposite sex, they won't accuse that person, but will accuse themselves of not being fair or of being wrong. It is highly likely that the experience of *injustice* that they live out with people of the opposite sex is, in fact, *betrayal*.

The more these wounds hurt us, the more it is normal and human to resent the parent we believe to be responsible for having made us suffer. Later, we transfer this resentment or this hatred onto people of the same sex as the parents we accuse of having hurt us. It's normal, for example, for a young boy to hate the father he feels has always rejected him. Later in life, he'll transfer that hatred onto other men or onto his son, by whom he will also feel rejected.

We also, subconsciously, resent our parents for having the same wound as we do. They therefore become models of someone suffering from our same wound, which forces us to look at ourselves. Subconsciously, we would prefer to have another model. This explains why we will do anything to avoid resembling them; we don't like what they reflect back to us. The wounds will only be healed through a thorough forgiveness process with ourselves and with our parents.

On the other hand, when any wound is lived out with someone of the sex opposite to the parent we hold responsible for our wound, we blame ourselves. It's at times like this that we are inclined to punish ourselves either by having an accident or with something that hurts our body. Human beings believe in punishment as a means to atone for their guilt. In actual fact, the spiritual law of love says just the opposite. The more we believe ourselves to be guilty, the more we punish ourselves and the more we attract the same situations. This means that the more we blame ourselves, the more we create the same problems. Feeling guilty makes forgiving ourselves, an important stage in the healing process, all the harder.

On top of the guilt, we also often feel ashamed when we accuse ourselves of having hurt someone or when others accuse us of having made them suffer from the wound or wounds that we haven't yet accepted. I speak in more detail about shame in the chapter on *humiliation*, because shame is seen most easily in *masochists*. But remember that everyone feels shame at one time or another. It is even more intense when we don't want to accept that we do to others what we wouldn't want others to do to us.

Serious abuse or violence indicates that those responsible have such deep wounds that they lose control. That's why I often say: There are no bad people in this world, there are only people who suffer. This doesn't mean that we can excuse them, but we can learn to have compassion for them, even if we don't agree. To condemn or blame them won't help them. The ability to feel compassion is one of the advantages of being conscious of our own wounds and those of others.

I've observed that it's rare for someone to have only one wound. I have already mentioned that I have two major wounds to heal in this lifetime: *injustice* and *betrayal*. I experience *injustice* with people of the same sex and *betrayal* with those of the opposite sex. As *injustice* is lived out with the parent of the same sex, I have realized that when I feel this emotion with someone of the female sex, I accuse her of being unfair. When the *injustice* comes from someone of the male sex, I will rather accuse myself of being unfair and I will be angry with myself. I sometimes even feel ashamed. I also perceive the *injustice* experienced with men as *betrayal*.

Both the *controller* and the *rigid* mask can, therefore, be seen in the bodies of those who, like me, suffer from the wounds of *injustice* and *betrayal*.

I've also observed that many people suffer the wounds of *rejection* and *abandonment* at the same time. They, therefore, wear both the *withdrawer* and the *dependent* masks. Sometimes the top half of the body reflects one wound and the bottom half, the other. With some people, there is a difference between the right side and the left. With time and practice, it becomes easier and easier to distinguish the masks at first sight. When we trust our intuition, our "inner eye" sees them very rapidly.

When people have *controller* type bodies but, at the same time, their bodies are soft and flabby, or they have *dependent* eyes, you can conclude that they suffer from the wounds of *betrayal* and *abandonment*.

There can, obviously, be other combinations. Others may have the fat body of a *masochist* and at the same time, be very straight, very *rigid*. We know, then, that they suffer from the wounds of *humiliation* and *injustice*.

People with the large *masochist* body, with the small legs and ankles of a *withdrawer,* are people who suffer from *humiliation* and *rejection*.

We can have three, four or even five wounds. One of the wounds may predominate whereas the others will be less obvious. They may also all be small. When a mask predominates, it's a sign that we use it more often than the others to protect ourselves. When the mask takes up very little space in our body, it's because we don't often feel the wound that is linked to this mask. Just because a mask is dominant, however, doesn't mean that the wound it hides is the one that most needs to be healed. On the contrary, we try to hide the wounds that make us suffer the most.

I've already mentioned in the previous chapters that we develop the mask of *rigidity* (*injustice*) and the *controller* mask (*betrayal*), which are masks of *control* and strength, to hide the wounds of *rejection*, *abandonment* or *humiliation*. The strength of these masks is used to hide that which hurts the most. This explains why we can frequently see one of the three masks appear with age; control has its limits. It's especially the mask of *rigidity*, due to its capacity to control, that is the most likely to hide another wound. People who are both *masochists* and *rigid* for example, will manage to control their weight for quite a while. When they can no longer control themselves, they put on weight.

Souls that come to Earth to heal the wound of *betrayal* will look for a strong, solid parent of the opposite sex, who knows how to take his or her place, who doesn't lose control and who isn't too emotional. At the same time, *controllers* want that parent to be understanding, to trust them and to satisfy all their expectations and their need for attention, which would prevent them from feeling abandoned and betrayed. If that parent shows indifference, they feel abandoned, but if they show any weakness or a lack of trust, they feel betrayed. If the parent of the opposite sex is too authoritarian, aggressive or violent, there will be a power struggle between them when the child becomes an adolescent, which will feed the wound of *betrayal* that they both suffer from.

We are specialists at finding all sorts of good reasons and explanations for why our bodies change. We can see that we are not ready to look at ourselves, and we find it especially hard to believe that the human body can be so intelligent. We don't want to admit that the slightest change in our physical bodies is a way to attract our attention to something we feel inside but don't want to see for the moment. If only we would realize that when our body decides to attract our attention to one of its inner behavior patterns, it is, in fact, our inner GOD using the physical body to tell us that we have everything we need at that moment to face whatever it is we are afraid of seeing. We choose to continue to hide our wounds and wear the masks we created, because we believe that by hiding them, our wounds will disappear.

Remember, we only wear our masks when we are afraid of suffering, of touching upon the wounds that our masks are supposed to protect. The behavior patterns described in the previous chapters are only used when we wear our masks. As soon as the mask is in place, we are no longer ourselves; we adopt the behavior linked to the mask we're wearing. It would be ideal to manage to recognize quickly which mask we've just put on, to identify the wound that we're trying to hide, and do that without judging or criticizing. We may change masks one or several times a day or we may wear the same mask for several months, several years even, before another wound comes to the surface.

When we realize what we're doing, we should be happy about our awareness and thank the incident or the person who touched the wound because that allowed us to see that it isn't yet healed. At least we are aware. Also, we must allow ourselves to be *human*. It is especially important that we give ourselves the necessary time to heal. When we can manage to say regularly to ourselves: *"I reacted like that because I put on such-and-such a mask,"* our healing process will be well advanced. I would like to remind you that it's very rare to have all the characteristics mentioned for one wound. Each character type is described to help you recognize yourself in some of the behavior patterns that are linked to your wound.

I will now recap ways to help you recognize when you, or someone else, has just put on a mask of protection:

• When the wound of *REJECTION* is activated, we wear the *withdrawer* mask. This makes us want to escape the

204

situation or the person we believe has rejected us, because we're afraid of panicking and feeling powerless. This mask may also convince us to become as invisible as possible by withdrawing into ourselves, by not saying or doing anything that might make us be rejected further. This mask makes us believe that we're not important enough to take our place in the world, that we don't have the same right as others to exist.

- When the wound of *ABANDONMENT* is activated, we wear the *dependent* mask. This makes us become like little children who need and seek attention by crying, complaining or being submissive because we believe we can't manage alone. This mask makes us go to great lengths to avoid being deserted or to receive more attention. It may even convince us to go as far as becoming ill or becoming the victim of various problems to obtain the support we're seeking.

- When the wound of *HUMILIATION* is activated, we wear the *masochist* mask. This mask makes us forget our needs to think only of the needs of others, and become good, generous people always ready to help out, even if we have to go beyond our limits. Without being asked, we also manage to take on a lot of other people's responsibilities and commitments. We do everything possible to make ourselves useful, and we do all that so we won't feel humiliated or put down. It's also important for us to make sure that we're not free. Each time our attitudes or actions are motivated by the fear of shame or *humiliation*, it's a sign that we're wearing our *masochist* mask.

- When we suffer from the wound of *BETRAYAL*, we wear the *controller* mask, which makes us become distrustful, skeptical, wary, authoritarian and intolerant because of our expectations. We do everything to show that we are strong and won't easily be taken advantage of. We particularly like to decide for others. This mask makes us do everything possible to avoid losing our good reputation; we'll even go as far as lying. We forget our needs and do whatever we can to make other people think that we are reliable and trustworthy. This mask also makes us project the image of self-confidence, even though we don't trust ourselves and frequently question our decisions or actions.

- When the wound of *INJUSTICE* is activated, we wear the mask of *rigidity*, which makes us appear cold, with dry and abrupt movements and tone of voice. Our bodies become rigid, just like our attitudes. This mask makes us become perfectionists and we feel a lot of anger, impatience and intolerance towards ourselves. We also criticize ourselves a great deal; we are very demanding and don't respect our limits. Each time we control ourselves in this way, each time we hold back and are hard on ourselves, it's a sign that we are wearing the mask of *rigidity*.

We wear a mask, not only each time we fear that someone is going to touch our wounds, but also when we fear the realization that we, too, activate other people's wounds. We, therefore, always wear the mask so that we'll be loved. We adopt behavior patterns that don't correspond to who we are. We become someone else. Because the behavior the mask dictates requires a great effort on our part, we expect a lot from others in return.

> *What we are and what we do must be the source of our well being and not the compliments, the gratitude, the appreciation or the support that others give us.*

Don't forget, however, how good the ego is at fooling us so that we don't become conscious of our wounds. The ego is convinced that if we become conscious of our wounds and eliminate them, we will no longer be protected and will suffer. I will now explain how each character type may be tricked by its ego.

› *Withdrawers* make themselves believe that they look after themselves and others well so that they don't feel all the *rejection* they've suffered.

› *Dependents* like to think they're independent and tell whoever wants to hear, how good they feel when they're alone and that they don't need anyone.

› *Masochists* convince themselves that they enjoy doing everything they do for others and that they really are listening to their needs by doing this. They excel at saying and thinking that everything's fine and at finding excuses for the situations or the people who have humiliated them.

› *Controllers* are convinced that they never lie, that they always keep their word and that they're frightened of no one.

› *Rigid* people like telling anyone and everyone how fair they are, that they have no problems in their lives, and they like to believe that they have a lot of friends who love them as they are.

We heal our inner wounds just like we heal physical wounds. Have you ever been so impatient to make a spot on your face disappear that you constantly played with it? What happened? The spot probably stayed a lot longer. That's what happens when we don't trust in the healing power of our own bodies. For a problem (whatever it may be) to disappear, you first have to accept it, to give it unconditional love rather than try to make it go away. Your deep wounds also need to be recognized, loved and accepted.

Let me remind you that unconditional love is accepting, even if you don't agree with or understand the reason for certain situations.

When we accept a wound or love the spots on our face, we accept that we create them for a specific reason and, more importantly, that we create them to help us. Instead of wanting to make our spots disappear, we should use them to become conscious of an aspect of ourselves that we don't want to see. In fact, those spots want to attract our attention to make us realize, among other things, that we are perhaps afraid of losing face in a given situation and that fear is preventing us from being ourselves. When we become aware of their usefulness, we will no longer see our spots in the same light. We could even end up thanking them. If we adopt this mental attitude, the "spots" will definitely disappear a lot more quickly because they will have been recognized and loved for their usefulness.

What must we accept? That what we fear others will do or what we reproach them for, we do to others, and above all, to ourselves.

Here are a few examples to show to what extent we can sometimes hurt ourselves.

⊙ When we suffer from *rejection*, we feed our wound each time we call ourselves worthless, good for nothing, each time we feel we make no difference in other people's lives, and each time we flee a situation.

⊙ If we suffer from *abandonment*, we feed the wound each time we abandon an important project, each time we fail to look after ourselves, and each time we fail to give ourselves the attention we need. We frighten others by hanging on to them too much and so lose them, to find ourselves alone once more. We make our bodies suffer a lot, creating illnesses to attract attention.

⊙ If we suffer from *humiliation*, we feed the wound each time we put ourselves down, each time we compare ourselves to others, each time we belittle ourselves and each time we criticize ourselves for being fat, no good, with no will power, for taking advantage, etc. We humiliate ourselves by wearing clothes that don't flatter us or by dirtying them. We make our bodies suffer by giving them too much food to digest and to assimilate. We make ourselves suffer by taking on other people's responsibilities, which deprives us of freedom and time to ourselves.

⊙ When we suffer from *betrayal*, we feed our wound by lying to ourselves, making ourselves believe things that are false, and not respecting our commitments to ourselves. We punish ourselves by doing everything ourselves because we don't trust others and we don't delegate. When we do delegate, we spend all our time and energy checking on what others are doing.

⊙ Those of us who suffer from *injustice* feed the wound by being too demanding of ourselves. We don't respect our limits so cause ourselves a lot of stress. We are critical of and unfair to ourselves. We find it hard to see our good qualities and what we do well. We suffer because we see only what we haven't yet done or the mistake that we made. We make ourselves suffer by having problems enjoying ourselves.

I mentioned earlier the importance of accepting our wounds unconditionally. It's also important to accept the masks that we have allowed our ego to create in order to protect us from those wounds. Loving and accepting a wound means acknowledging it, knowing that we have come back to earth to heal this type of wound and accepting that our egos want to protect us by creating a mask. We can then thank ourselves for having had the courage to create and maintain a mask that contributed to our survival.

Today, however, this mask harms us more than it helps. The time has come to decide that we can survive, even if we feel hurt. We are no longer little children; we can now deal with our wounds as adults with more experience, maturity, and with a different vision of life. From now on, we can decide to love ourselves.

I mentioned in the first chapter that the creation of a wound goes through four stages. In the first stage we are ourselves. In the second, we experience pain, discovering that we can't be ourselves because that doesn't suit the adults around us. (Unfortunately, adults don't realize that their children are trying to discover who they are and, instead of letting them be themselves, they spend their time telling their children who they should be.) In the third stage, we revolt at having felt so much pain. This is the time during which children have fits of anger and resist their parents. The fourth and last stage brings resignation. It is at this point that we decide to create a mask to try not to disappoint others and, above all, to shield us from the suffering that results from not being accepted as ourselves.

The healing process will be complete when we manage to reverse the four stages, beginning at the fourth and returning to the first, where we become ourselves once more. The first stage in this process is to become aware of the mask (or masks) you wear. Use as your guide the five preceding chapters that describe each of the wounds.

You will have reached the second stage when you start to feel resistance while reading these chapters or when you refuse to accept your responsibility, preferring to accuse others for your suffering. Remember that it's normal for all human beings to resist when they discover aspects of themselves that they don't like. People react differently during this stage. Some are more resistant than others. The intensity of your revolt will depend on your level of acceptance, the depth of your wound at the time you become conscious of what is happening inside you, and your willingness to change and heal.

During the third stage, you must give yourself the right to have suffered and to have resented one or both your parents. If you can feel how deeply the child in you suffered, you'll have more compassion for that inner child. The more compassion you have, the more profound this stage will be. During this stage, you can also let go of what you felt towards your parents by feeling compassion for their suffering as well.

Finally, in the fourth stage you become yourself once more; you stop believing that you still need to wear your masks to protect you. You accept that life is full of experiences that are there to help you learn what is beneficial and intelligent for you. This is called LOVING YOURSELF. As love has great healing and energizing powers, prepare yourself to observe several transformations in your life: illnesses may disappear or your physical body may change, and your relationships with others will definitely be transformed.

Remember, love has nothing to do with what we do or possess. Loving ourselves means allowing ourselves to be as we are in the moment; accepting, even if we do to others what we reproach them for doing.

Real love is the experience of being yourself.

Loving ourselves is, therefore, accepting that we will sometimes hurt others unintentionally by rejecting, abandoning, humiliating, betraying and being unjust to them. This is the first and most important step towards healing our wounds.

To help you reach this stage, I suggest that at the end of each day, you write down all that has happened that day. Ask yourself which mask got the better of you by causing you to react in a given situation, or by dictating your behavior towards others or towards yourself. Then take the time to write down your observations and remember to comment on how you felt. When you've done that, forgive yourself and give yourself the right to have used the mask, knowing that, at that time, you sincerely thought it was the only way to protect yourself. Let me remind you that if you feel guilty and criticize yourself, you'll continue to react in the same way when a similar situation occurs.

Without acceptance, there can be no transformation.

How can we know if we're really accepting? When we know that our behavior is part of being human and accept the consequences, whatever they may be. This notion of responsibility is fundamental if we really want to accept ourselves. The fact that we are human means that we can't please everyone and we have a right to certain human reactions others may dislike.

Acceptance is therefore the trigger that starts the healing process.

In fact, to your great surprise, you'll discover that the more you allow yourself to betray, reject, abandon, humiliate or be unjust, the less you'll do it. Surprising, wouldn't you say? If you've been following my teaching for awhile, you won't be surprised. I'm not asking you to believe me or to understand, because this can't be understood intellectually. It needs to be experienced.

I repeat this great spiritual law of love in all my books, workshops and conferences because it needs to be heard several times before it can be integrated. When you give yourself the right to do to others what you fear they'll do to you (which is why you created one or several masks to protect yourself), it will be a lot easier for you to give others the right to occasionally behave in ways that awaken your wounds.

Let's say, for example, a father decides to disinherit one of his daughters because she rebelled against his wishes. She didn't want to study and become "someone worthwhile" as he expected her to because she was very talented. The daughter may perceive this decision as *betrayal, abandonment, rejection, humiliation* or *injustice*, depending on what wound she has come to solve on Earth. I knew a woman whose father disinherited her, and she felt betrayed; she would never have believed that her father would go so far. She hoped that her father would accept her choices and finally admit that she had the right to do what she wanted with her life. The only way for her to heal this wound and stop attracting situations in which she feels betrayed by the men in her life is, first of all, to realize that her father also felt she betrayed him. The fact that his daughter didn't live up to his expectations was a form of *betrayal* in his eyes. He could say that after all he did for her, she should have been grateful, should have become a more responsible woman and done him honor. He also hoped that she would come back one day, say that he was right and make honorable amends.

What happened between the father and his daughter shows us that he also felt betrayed by his mother (and his mother felt he betrayed her). When we find out what our parents went through with their parents when they were young, we realize that history repeats itself from generation to generation and will continue to do so until real forgiveness has begun. This also helps us to feel more compassion and understanding for our parents. Once you have discovered your wounds, I strongly suggest you check with your parents to see if they have the same ones. Remember that they won't necessarily have had experiences identical to yours, but they will have suffered the same wounds and accused their parents of the same things you do.

This all becomes easier when we stop accusing ourselves for behavior patterns that are dictated by our wounds, and when we accept that it's all part of being human. We then feel much more at ease to speak about it to our parents without worrying about feeling accused. That also helps our parents reveal themselves more fully, because they don't feel judged. When you speak to them about all of this, you help them go through their own forgiveness process with *their* parents. It also allows them to be human, to have wounds that sometimes make them react and behave in ways that are the contrary to the way they would like to be.

When you speak to the parents who awakened a wound in you, I suggest you check with them to see if they also suffered in the same way with *you*. If, for example, you are a woman and you tell your mother you have felt rejected by her ever since you were a teenager, ask her if she too felt rejected by you. That will allow her to free emotions that she has held back for a long time and that might even be subconscious. Thanks to you, your mother might become more aware of her own feelings. You could then ask her to speak about what she went through with her mother. (This example is also valid for men with their fathers.) For more details on real forgiveness, I suggest you read my other books where this process is explained more fully.[1]

I would like to remind you that if you idealized the parent with whom you lived out a wound, and especially if you considered him or her to be a saint, it's absolutely normal that you find it hard to allow yourself to have resented that parent. You must know that if you felt that this parent was a saint, it's because he/she probably suffered from the wound of *injustice* and managed to control himself (herself) enough not to show what he/she was feeling. *Masochist* types also often seem to be saints because of their great devotion.

Here are a few ways you can recognize that your wounds are being healed.

---

1   *Listen to Your Body, Your Best Friend on Earth*, *Listen to Your Body, Part 2* and *Your Body's Telling You " Love Yourself !"*

> Your wound of *REJECTION* is being healed when you take your 'place' more and more, when you dare to assert yourself. On top of that, if someone seems to forget that you exist, you still manage to feel good. Fewer situations arise where you're afraid of panicking.

> Your wound of *ABANDONMENT* is being healed when you feel good even when alone, and need less attention from others. Life is less dramatic. You feel more and more like undertaking projects, and even if others don't support you, you are able to continue.

> Your wound of *HUMILIATION* is being healed when you take the time to check your needs before saying yes to others. You take on less and you feel freer. You stop creating limits for yourself. You are also able to ask for things without feeling that you are being a bother or worse, a real pain in the neck.

> Your wound of *BETRAYAL* is being healed when you are no longer so upset if someone or something interferes with your plans. You let go more easily. I would like to specify that letting go means to stop being attached to the results, to stop wanting everything to go the way you have planned it. You no longer want to be the center of attention. When you are very proud of yourself after accomplishing something, you can still feel good even if others don't acknowledge you.

> Your wound of *INJUSTICE* is being healed when you allow yourself to be less perfect, to make mistakes without feeling angry or criticizing yourself. You allow

yourself to show your sensitivity, to cry in front of others without losing control and without fearing the judgement of others.

Another marvelous advantage to healing our wounds is that we become self-reliant rather than emotionally *dependent*. Self-reliance is the ability to know what we want and do what's necessary to obtain it. When we need help, we know how to ask for it without expecting one particular person to help us. When someone disappears from our lives, we don't say: *"What's going to become of me now that I'm all alone?"* We may feel sad, but we know deep down that we can survive alone.

I hope that the discovery of your wounds will allow you to feel compassion for yourself and bring you greater inner peace so that you are no longer ruled by anger, shame, or rancor. I realize it isn't necessarily easy to face that which hurts us. We, as human beings, have invented so many different ways to repress our painful memories that it's very tempting to use one of them.

On the other hand, the more we repress our painful memories, the deeper we bury them into our subconscious. Then, one day, when we can no longer continue to bury them and we reach the limits of our self-control, these memories come to the surface and our pain is even more difficult to handle. By confronting our wounds and healing them, all the energy we used to repress and hide our pain will finally be released and we'll be able to use it much more productively; in other words, by remaining ourselves we can create our life as we would like it to be.

As your wounds heal and your masks diminish, you will be happy to discover your true self. Following are the positive aspects, the strengths within us that are linked to the different character types. These strengths are always there, buried in each of us. But, as previously mentioned, they are all too often ignored or are badly used because we accord such importance to our masks; and all that to avoid seeing or feeling our wounds. Once our wounds are healed, in other words when we are ourselves, without fear, this is what is likely to surface:

Behind the mask of withdrawal (wound of rejection) hide people with great stamina who are capable of taking on a lot.

... Resourceful, very gifted when it comes to creating, inventing, imagining;

... Special aptitude for working alone;

... Efficient; think of countless details;

... Able to react, to take necessary action in emergencies;

... Don't need others at all costs. Can very well withdraw and be happy alone.

Behind the mask of dependence (wound of abandonment) hide skillful people who know how to ask for what they want.

... Know what they want. Tenacious, persevere with their requests;

... Don't give up when they're determined to obtain something;

... Good actors. Know how to get other people's attention;

... Naturally cheerful, playful and sociable, they reflect joy;

... Help others because they take an interest and understand how they feel;

... Put their psychic gifts to good use when their fears have been mastered;

... Often have artistic talent;

... Although sociable, they need moments of solitude to recuperate.

Behind the mask of masochism (wound of humiliation) hide bold, adventurous, competent people.

... Know and respect their needs;

... Sensitive to the needs of others, able to respect other people's freedom;

... Good mediators, conciliators. Likely to put things into perspective;

... Jovial, like pleasure and putting others at ease;

... Naturally generous, helpful, altruistic;

… Talented organizers. Know their talents;

… Sensual, know how to enjoy themselves in love;

… Have great dignity; they are very proud.

Behind the mask of control (the wound of betrayal) hide people with leadership qualities.

… Through their strength, they are reassuring and protective;

… Very talented. Sociable and good actors;

… Good at speaking in public;

… See and bring out people's talents by helping them to acquire more self-confidence;

… Ability to delegate, which helps others feel more capable;

… Rapidly know how others feel and put things into perspective by making them laugh;

… Quickly go from one thing to another and manage many things at the same time;

… Make decisions quickly. Find what they need and surround themselves with the people they need to be able to act;

… Capable of high performance at several levels;

... Trust in the Universe and their inner strength. Ability to let go completely.

Behind the mask of rigidity (wound of injustice) hide creative people, with a lot of energy and a great capacity for work.

... Methodical, excellent at producing work that demands great precision;

... Concerned, very gifted at taking care of and checking details;

... Able to simplify, to explain clearly, to teach;

... Very sensitive, know easily what others feel;

... Know what they need to know at the time they need to know it;

... Find the right person to do specific jobs, and the exact, precise thing to say;

... Enthusiastic, lively and dynamic;

... Don't need others to feel good;

... Like *withdrawers*, in an emergency, they know what to do and do it themselves;

... Manage to face difficult situations.

As you can see, some strengths appear in more than one wound, which increases them ten-fold. They therefore become extraordinary assets with which you can demonstrate what you want. By recognizing the unique person you are, you can't fail to be a source of energizing inspiration.

Don't forget that we are on this planet to remember who we are: we are all GOD, experiencing life on earth. Unfortunately, while living all our incarnations since the beginning of time, we've forgotten this along the way.

To remember who we are, we must become conscious of what we are not. We are *not* our wounds, for example. Each time we suffer, it's because we believe that we are what we are not. When our body is ill, we are *not* the illness, we are a person experiencing an energy blockage in part of our body, and we call this experiencing "illness." When we suffer from guilt because we have just rejected another or because we have just been unfair, we believe we *are rejection* or *injustice*. We are not the experience; we are GOD experiencing life on a material planet.

LIFE IS MARVELOUS AND PERFECT.

A continuous succession of processes brings us to our only reason for being, which is to

REMEMBER WE ARE GOD.

The creation of our masks expresses the greatest betrayal of all: having forgotten that we are GOD.

We'll finish this book with a poem by the Swedish poet Hjalmar Sôderberg.

We all want to be loved,
Failing that, to be admired,
Failing that, to be feared,
Failing that, to be hated and despised.

We want to awaken an emotion in others,
Whatever it may be.

The soul trembles in front of nothingness
and seeks contact at all costs.

ÉCOUTE TON CORPS
International

Improving the quality of life!

The
LISTEN TO YOUR BODY
workshop

improves the quality of your life!

LISTEN TO YOUR BODY
workshop

Start enjoying life!

The dynamic and powerful teachings of the *"Listen to Your Body"* workshop are aimed at all people who are interested in their personal growth.

For the past twenty years, this workshop has provided people with a vital source of knowledge as well as a solid foundation in order to be more in harmony with themselves. Year after year, the startling results and enriching transformations achieved by over 25,000 people who attended this workshop are truly astounding.

Thanks to this workshop, thousands of people are no longer putting up with life; they are living it! They have regained control over their lives and are using the wealth of personal power within them to create the lives they really want for themselves. The rewards are far greater than could be imagined.

The *"Listen to Your Body"* workshop is a unique and comprehensive teaching which has tangible effects at all levels: physical, emotional, mental and spiritual.

Benefits of this workshop according to previous participants are:

- ✓ greater self-confidence;
- ✓ better communication with others;
- ✓ better judgement enabling a conscious choice between love and fear;
- ✓ an ability to forgive and let go of the past;
- ✓ a direct contact with your personal power and creativity;
- ✓ a revolutionary but simple technique to discover the real causes of illnesses and health problems;
- ✓ greater physical vitality;
- ✓ and much more!

If you would like to organize a workshop in your town/city, contact us for further information.

1102 La Sallette believe, Bellefeuille (Quebec) J0R 1A0 CANADA
Tel: 450-431-5336 or 514-875-1930, Toll free: 1-800-361-3834
Fax: 450-431-0991; E-MAIL: info@ecoutetoncorps.com
www.ecoutetoncorps.com

Books from the same author

Listen to your best friend on Earth, your body

LISE BOURBEAU takes you by the hand and, step by step, leads you beyond "packing your own parachute", to taking that step back into the clear, refreshing stream of life that flows from the Universal Source. She gives you the tools, not only to fix what is wrong in your life, but to build a solid foundation for your inner house - a foundation that extends as far as the global village. In this book, she helps you build an intimate, rewarding and powerful relationship with the most important person in your life - yourself.

Your body's telling you: Love yourself!

Lise Bourbeau has compiled 20 years of research in the field of metaphysics and it's physical manifestations in the body and brought it all to the forefront in this user-friendly reference guide, Your body's telling you: Love yourself! Since 1982, she has worked successfully with over 15,000 people, helping them to unearth the underlying causes of specific illnesses and diseases.

"I am certain that any physical problem is simply the outward manifestation of dis-ease on psychological and/or emotional levels. The physical body is responding to this imbalance and warning of the need to return to the path of love and harmony."

Cover to cover, the reader discovers a most powerful tool, as he becomes his own healer. The reference material, a comprehensive guide to the causes of over 500 illnesses and diseases, is a succinct and visionary work that is truly and literally a labor of love.

Heal your wounds and find your true self

Do you sometimes feel that you are going around in circles in your personal growth? Do you occasionally see a problem re-emerge, thinking you had solved it? Perhaps it's because you're not looking in the right place.

This new book by Lise Bourbeau, as concrete as her others, demonstrates that all problems, whether physical, emotional or mental, stem from five important wounds: *rejection, abandonment, humiliation, betrayal* and *injustice*. This book contains detailed descriptions of these wounds and of the masks we've developed to hide them.

This book will allow you to set off on the path that leads to complete healing, the path that leads to your ultimate goal: your true self.